THE FELLOWSHIP OF THE KING

THE FELLOWSHIP OF THE KING

The Quest for Community and Purpose

Liam Goligher

Authentic
LIFESTYLE

Contents

Foreword

Perhaps no movie series has been as eagerly awaited as the blockbuster trilogy *The Lord of the Rings*. In the first of the series, the general public were reintroduced to a word that has gone out of fashion in everyday speech. An unlikely group of individuals – racially mixed, culturally different and variously gifted – are thrown together into a common life with a common mission, a common enemy and a common destiny. The sum of the whole of that *fellowship* is found to be greater than that of the individual parts. In a modern day *Pilgrim's Progress*, Pilgrim (Frodo Baggins) is joined by others in his task to take the One Ring to the terrible land of Mordor – the only place in which it can be destroyed. Even when they are separated from one another by circumstances, there is evidence of an ongoing allegiance to each other and to the task. The strength of their fellowship has a palpable effect on audiences, who are drawn to the depth and strength of their relationship with each other.

For modern men and women there is little of the kind of fellowship modelled in *The Fellowship of the Ring*. There is a sense of disconnectedness, in which people often appear quite isolated. Robert D. Putnam has researched the breakdown of community in the United

States[1] but his conclusions apply far more widely. He speaks of the loss of 'social capital' – the invisible glue that makes our society work – and the consequences of this. Let me pick out one element in this social richness at random – networks of relationships. He points out

> Social networks help you stay healthy... For example stroke victims who had strong support networks functioned better after the stroke, and recovered more physical capacities, than did stroke victims with thin social networks. Older people who are involved with clubs, volunteer work and local politics consider themselves to be in better health than do uninvolved people, even after accounting for socio-economic status, demographics, level of medical care use, and years of retirement.[2]

Of course the loss of community affects more than our physical health; it erodes mental and spiritual well-being also. Any renewal of social engagement is a commendable goal but our humanity cries out for more than this. In the past we have looked to national, racial and economic factors to give us our sense of belonging, but none of these have satisfied our inner craving to find true community.

So imagine belonging – belonging to a group of people who accept you for who you are, who share your values and sense of purpose; people who are bound to you by more than social capital! In this book we hope to point to the attractive and compelling vision of fellowship presented in the Christian Scriptures. In fact, we believe that the vision of fellowship to be found there is one of the great 'apologies' or compelling reasons for Christian faith. The Bible paints a picture of a radical and world-changing new community in which there is unconditional acceptance, personal value, a shared mission and a common destiny. I have said 'we' for this has been very much a joint venture with my editor – I am grateful to Colin Duriez for his hard work in making this manuscript fit for publication and without whose help this would never have made it from my study to the publisher! I should add that the real life stories we have used in the book have usually been fictionalised and modified to protect identities.

For Western society, the twenty-first century is an era of cultural dislocation and social disintegration. People, finding it harder than ever to relate with others, feel anonymous, isolated and independent. Tellingly, Michael Schluter and David Lee write:

> We find ourselves scattered too far and moving too fast to maintain a strong base of counter relationships. Relationship is less and less a matter of sharing the same patch of earth and the same block of air. We meet many more people, but less frequently. We still have friends and families, but on the whole these relationships are fewer, more intermittent and less stable. Instead we feel millions of tiny threads tying us into general and indirect relationship with people we never touch or talk to, people who as individuals we know nothing about nor ever will. This has a profound effect on the way we live. It means that in 'the mega-community', we live among strangers.[3]

But what does the Bible have to say about the breakdown of relationships, society's loss of community and our search for love? After all, it was written in a very different world which experienced the extended family and integral community – a world away from modernity and our crisis of social change.

In answer, this book is essentially a biblical exploration of the Greek word, *koinonia*, usually translated in

our English Bibles as 'fellowship' or 'communion.'
The book's principal premise is that God, who enjoys
koinonia within his own nature, created us to enjoy
koinonia with himself and with our fellow human beings.
This is the key that unlocks our humanity. But how may
we enjoy what we are created to enjoy? John expresses
the biblical good news like this: 'We proclaim to you
what we have seen and heard, so that you also may have
[*koinonia*] with us. And our [*koinonia*] is with the Father
and with his Son, Jesus Christ.'[4]

1

Who wants to be alone?

Emma has known Glyn for twenty years. For the last seven of those years she has been his girlfriend. He has been in the habit of calling her every few days.

More than a week passes without a call. Emma begins to worry. Then she hears in a passing conversation that someone overdosed a few days before in a busy street in the City of London. Fearing the worst, she rings the public phone box where she knows other people who sleep rough hang out. The person who answers hurriedly confers with others and then tells her that the lad who died fits Glyn's description.

As he carries no identification, Glyn is one of around a hundred people a people a year likely to be buried in unmarked graves.[5] Fortunately, Emma is able to establish his identity after the interment and his family eventually is tracked down. Many others are not. One victim of a huge fire at Kings Cross underground station in 1988 remains unidentified to this day.

Homeless in life, anonymous in death, the fate of many young people today writes large the horror in today's society of being lost in the crowd.

When Greta Garbo famously remarked 'I want to be alone,'[6] she echoed our occasional yearning to rid ourselves of the hustle and bustle of everyday life. But all men and women, especially Hollywood actresses, find that regular contact with other human beings is like the air we breathe – something that cannot be lived without. From the new-born baby's first struggled gasps, to the dying person's final breath, human beings are *social* creatures.

Friendship, sexual love, marriage, family ties, the bond between parent and child, even having traceable next of kin – such is the oxygen of human life. Even if people do not experience all the possibilities of human relationship, without others in their lives they die. Sometimes the death is inward and not easily visible at first.

Our social nature is nowhere more apparent than with children. Child development psychologists have found that infants, if abandoned, first protest by screaming, then they quietly withdraw, and finally, after about two weeks, they become detached and apathetic. Subjecting children to sustained periods of solitude will probably harm their emotional development: their play with other children will be joyless and lacking emotional involvement.[7] Fifty years ago, René Spitz observed that infants may actually die if they are not played with, talked to, held, stroked, and 'loved,'[8] and later another psychologist wrote that it was possible, after all, to die of a 'broken heart.'[9]

The book and film, *Harry Potter and the Philosopher's Stone*, aroused the sympathy of many children. There the dastardly Dursley family consigns the hapless orphan Harry to live in a cupboard under the stairs. Happily, Harry finds community and acceptance as he attends Hogwarts School. The book was written by J.K. Rowling, then a single mother who felt keenly the fracturing of social relations as she struggled to bring up her little daughter.

Not just children suffer ill effects from solitude. Social contact is a powerful need for all ages. Twenty per cent of adults admit to feeling lonely at any one time,[10] and in a recent survey, one in five Americans bemoaned the fact that they did not have a friend with whom they could discuss a personal problem.

People can feel 'alone in a crowd,' even as they travel on a train packed with thousands of commuters, or are crammed shoulder-to-shoulder with ten other people in an elevator. Loneliness is obviously different from solitude! Very few people want to buy a yacht and sail, alone, around the world, but almost everyone welcomes the prospect of a temporary respite from the hustle and bustle of everyday life. This may be a walk in the hills, or an evening at home watching a favourite football game on television.

In the Hollywood blockbuster, *Cast Away*, Tom Hanks plays Chuck Noland, a globetrotting, workaholic Federal Express service manager. He sets off to Malaysia on a work assignment but his aircraft crashes and he is washed up on a desert island in the South Pacific with only his wits and the contents of a few rescued FedEx packages for survival. The film is more than a remake of Daniel Defoe's famous novel. In *Robinson Crusoe*, the eponymous hero finds a trusty friend, Friday, whereas in *Cast Away* Chuck Noland is completely and devastatingly alone. For Western world viewers, the drama is made all the more heady and intoxicating because every second of Chuck Noland's life had been driven and controlled by the precise ticking of a corporate clock. One reviewer wrote: 'The most poignant moments for me were less those which depicted his attempts to stay physically alive in an unknown and inhospitable world, but rather his enduring need for companionship in order to sustain life … Alone there is no reason to live … Alone there is no life … Alone he cannot exist.'[11]

Whatever else *Cast Away* achieves, it raises real questions about the isolation and individualism of society. Why do more and more people 'choose' to live alone, when, in a survey carried out by a newspaper, they admit that it requires a conscious and continual effort? Why do people feel more alone, anonymous and independent, when more and more people live in closer proximity to each other?[12] And why are people migrating away from city centres, only to experience a greater sense of isolation in the suburbs?

A *Time* magazine article[13] is among many that have traced the sociological impact of the 'move to the suburbs.' Living in the city centre, young mothers had been able to work and rear their children with the support of the extended family and neighbours. In the suburbs, despite the comfort of the new family home, young mothers suffer from many isolating effects: their partners are away from the home for longer, the working day extended by tedious commuting; their support networks are missing, and their children, lacking playmates, have become bored. One of the few benefits of these changes is that it has unsettled many people, causing them to challenge the direction our society has taken.

Expectations of romantic love

This rethinking of social change can be seen in many marriages. A mark of our society is the huge weight it places upon romantic love. Second marriages have increased dramatically and have caused many who have experienced it to reconsider this dominant emphasis on romance. False expectations of romantic love lead to disappointment in marriage, and subsequently to divorce. People who marry again have an awareness of this. They speak of 'trying harder this time' and 'not messing up a second time.' In the face of a shift in our culture away from commitment, entry into second marriage often takes considerable courage.

The circumstances of second marriage make the challenge all the greater. There is the 'emotional baggage' of the experiences of the first marriage and the complexities of children and financial obligations (from the first marriage) to contend with. Loyalties are constantly tested and thus second marriages are even more likely to fail.

Those in second marriages, however, are often determined to make the new relationship work and have learnt to make priorities of other things – such as financial support and emotional stability – over the dream of a romantic idyll. Some painfully conclude that, in retrospect, they could have saved their first marriage if only they had realised the realities of commitment at the time.

Lost in the crowd

The isolation we increasingly feel is emphasised if we live alone. The number of people who do so has increased considerably over the last fifteen years.[14] There are many reasons for this massive change in the way many of us live: women have greater financial independence; people settle into relationships later and therefore often rent or buy a property alone in their twenties; more people get divorced and find themselves living alone in their thirties and forties (there's a growing market for one bedroom flats in the City for middle-aged men returning to the single lifestyle after their marriage has failed and they have to leave their commuter-belt house and family) and people are living longer.

For those who live alone there is no community or fellowship in their day-to-day home life. For many, the only callers at their home are for parcel delivery, checking the meter, or selling double glazing. Many of their phone calls may be from telephone sales operatives, plying their wares. All deeper contact with others must therefore be beyond the four walls of their home.

Life in segments

Urban life paradoxically underscores our growing isolation from each other. Perhaps ninety per cent of the population in the United Kingdom lives in urban areas, a pattern reflected in all Westernised countries. The vast majority of us live in what appear to be communities – in streets, with neighbours either side and, for many, people above and below us too. Think of all those little households so close to each other. Yet how much do we really have to do with our neighbours? The honest answer has to be that it is increasingly little.

Why is there this increasing aloneness? There are in fact numerous causes, all of which interact to increase the grip of isolation. They boil down to the fact that we have fewer reasons to mix with the local community. We travel further to our place of employment, rather than work locally; we labour longer hours; more mums return to work when their children reach school-age; we buy our groceries at the out-of-town supermarket rather than visit the local shops; we encourage our children to stay indoors rather than to play in the street and mix with neighbours' children; we drive our children to school and life is more transient as people move from one community to another at different stages of their lives.

Increasingly we live our lives and relate to others in discrete pockets. We go to work and see our colleagues; we head off to the gym (which may be a car journey away) and see other people training; we collect our children from school and see other parents; we go to the pub to meet our friends and we visit our own parents for the occasional weekend – and often they are at separate locations! We relate to each segment of our lives quite separately. There is very little cross over between the various groups we encounter.

Consequently, we show different facets of ourselves to the different groups of people we know. We feel that very few people know the 'real' or 'complete' us. This reveals itself when problems arise. We talk of having no one to talk to when we face a crisis, as in, 'no one I know really understands my situation'; we lack confidence that any friends can identify with our perspective on the situation. Interestingly, we are more likely to confide in those we work with – at least, we feel, these are the people with whom we spend the bulk of our time.

Technology – a false friend?

The recent century's explosion of technology, rather than alleviating our loss of community, has continued to erode the bonds of neighbourly interdependence. Who needs to borrow a cup of sugar when they have a microwave and the latest fresh-chilled ready-meals? The telephone, thought by many to promote social interaction, has contributed to a reduced dependence on face-to-face communication and one-to-one social interactions, and long hours in front of a television have, for many, increased their sense of seclusion and aloneness.

Perhaps the most isolating technology of all, however, is the Internet. In an endeavour to cut costs, improve operational efficiency and deliver competitive advantage, many large corporations are exploiting the power and reach of the Internet to replace their expensive city-centre buildings with low-cost networks of home-workers. But for many workers, the office was the place where most of their day-to-day social interactions occurred. By contrast, working alone at home, in front of a personal computer, is isolating and secluding.

There are other ways that the Internet heightens aloneness: shoppers can purchase their weekly groceries without leaving their homes; adolescents can spend hours combating the latest virtual adversary without leaving their bedrooms and even gamblers can wager away their money without talking to another human being.

Yet our widespread use of the Internet has demonstrated that our appetite for community remains the same. We are social animals and instinctively seek the company of others. In absence of real community, virtual communities are emerging. The rise of the Internet has emphasised this as people join online clubs and talk in chat rooms.

The desire to connect with others is also evident in the growth of mobile phones. Of course, there are numerous practical reasons for owning them, but look at how people actually use their phones. Think about the number of conversations you overhear on the bus or the train – the excuse for calling may be practical but the conversation is far more social, even if it is only to say that John is 'just on the train and about to leave Manchester.'

Furthermore, consider the phenomenal increasing in texting, the facility that mobile phone operators originally thought of merely as 'nice to have.' Little did they predict how people would seize on it as a novel and flexible way to relate to each other.

Some people say that text messaging avoids contact or dialogue but I would argue that it has enabled people to stay close to those they care about. Wives talk about the romantic messages they receive from their husbands as they travel on the train home from work – things they had long ago forgotten actually to say to each other. Others talk about rekindling friendships with a subtle text message – rather than having to take the plunge of the first phone call.

Other examples of people trying to relate to, and have fellowship with, others are demonstrated in successes in the TV ratings. *Big Brother*, Channel 4's reality TV show, provided the nation with a focus, with currency, with something to talk about and share views on. Without community, we lack points of common knowledge, be it events or individuals – and this is where television is beginning to fill the gap. During the hype of *Big Brother* seasons, it is not unusual to sit on the train and hear people discussing Jade or Kate (characters on the show) as if they were people they know well.

Similarly, and perhaps more penetratingly, TV soaps are also stepping into the community vacuum. People use the characters, situations and experiences of TV soaps not only as a common world to share but also as a way of learning about and equipping themselves for the experiences life can throw in their path. This may sound extreme but it is not unusual for parents to say they use TV soap storylines as a way of broaching and exploring difficult issues with their children, such as drug-taking, sex and relationships.

This use of TV programming may seem simply indicative of contemporary lifestyles. There is something more sinister however about relying on a contrived community;

the experience is not real, but can be all too convincing. Witnessing scripted experience cannot replace sharing with those who are genuinely encountering life's trials and tribulations. Scripted experience almost always incorporates a fictional safety net which real life does not offer. Scripted experience can be up for scrutiny, criticism and discussion with no real consequence, no responsibility. Connection with other people and real life experiences is not so disposable or so safely ignored.

Loneliness – an issue for all of us

With urban areas rapidly expanding and megacities emerging, we find ourselves more, not less, isolated. Scattered and increasingly mobile, we are cast adrift from community and enduring relationships. As Michael Schluter and David Lee observed, 'We live among strangers.'[15]

Unique however in our modern world is a new kind of loneliness – cosmic aloneness. This is much more than an awareness of the vastness of the universe. Even educated people in the Middle Ages were aware of the immensity of the heavens, even though they had no photographs of early galaxies from the further reaches of the universe. As people grapple with their very identity, the quest to find life elsewhere in the universe has become urgent. Carl Sagan's novel, *Contact*, was made into a successful film starring Jodie Foster. It tells the story of a scientist, Dr Ellie Arroway, who is a materialist. From her earliest days she has had an unquenchable wonder about the world around her and the cosmos above her that revealed itself at night. She commits her life and career to the search for extra-terrestrial intelligence (SETI). It is, in effect, a religious quest.

Twenty-first century Western society belongs to an era of cultural dislocation, social disintegration and increasing loneliness on a scale never witnessed before in human history. But what is loneliness? It is difficult to define with precision, though most writers recognise that there are different types of loneliness. There is social loneliness, when people miss some kind of social contact, such as a close friend, an old work colleague or a member of the family. There is emotional loneliness, when contact with other human beings lacks intimacy, often experienced by those in an 'empty-shell' marriage. There is also *spiritual* loneliness, when people feel a sense of separation from God and there is existential loneliness, where people are shaken by an awareness or self-knowledge about their individual sense of separateness.

In an attempt better to understand loneliness, some writers[16] categorise its emotions. There is *desperation*, the feeling of helplessness, anxiety and fear; *depression*, the feeling of emptiness, *impatient boredom*, the sense of restlessness, often accompanied by anger; and finally *self-criticism*, those feelings that emerge from low self-esteem – I'm ugly, I'm stupid, I'm too fat, I'm worthless, no one would ever want me.

Psychologists and sociologists may be able to distinguish between different types of loneliness, but it is far harder to categorise its *causes*. Why are human beings lonely? Ostensibly, there are hundreds of answers. The breakdown of a relationship causes loneliness, especially a romantic relationship.[17] Cultural values of competition and independence can increase people's sense of isolation. Traumatic childhood experiences can cause loneliness: a child who lacks the love and affirmation of its parents will often develop into an adult who feels unneeded, unwanted and different from others. Apparently innocent circumstances can cause loneliness:

a recent house move, a change in job, a cancelled holiday or a change in life-style.

Thousands of books have been written to help people overcome loneliness, but very few seem to halt the long-term, gloomy slide into a lowered sense of self-esteem, which leads, in turn, to increased loneliness then depression. Many therapists talk about the 'scary dread' of being alone and warn about the enormous damage that loneliness is exacting on society. M.E. Macdonald wrote, 'The real menace to life in the world today is not the nuclear bomb but the fact of *proximity* without *community*.'[18]

Is there an answer to loneliness? Many existentialists do not seem to think so. Clark Moustakas[19] points out, somewhat pessimistically, that aloneness is the human condition; men and women are born alone, they direct their lives alone, and in the same profound sense, they die alone. But do human beings have to grudgingly accept loneliness as an illness, only treating its severest symptoms?

The most important premise of this book is that the Christian message has something hugely important to say about this increasingly urgent predicament. The Bible claims to have a lot to say about our sense of separation, seclusion and aloneness. Though written in a very different world, it addresses our deepest human quest. It recognises that people need each other as well as needing God, and that 'aloneness' is not the will of God, especially for those that have embarked on the Christian life.

This is why the following chapters are *biblical* studies. Together, they offer a fresh approach to men and women's search for community and purpose. What is God's assessment of the *causes* of loneliness, and what remedies does God offer to those who suffer isolation?

Greta: Isolation in the community

Greta is in her mid-sixties. Three years ago she was widowed. One night her husband could not sleep. He got up to make them a cup of tea. Soon after drinking the tea, he turned over on to his side. Greta heard him make a strange breathing noise. She asked if he was all right. When he didn't answer, she put on the light and found him dead. She has repeated this story many times as it plays back in her mind. She finds it impossible to draw herself out of her grief. She has withdrawn into her large Victorian home (in a salubrious London village) and spends her time reading the newspapers. She has strong views on the state of the country but, beyond this, refuses to participate in the world around her. Her local community is aesthetically inviting but, in personality, hollow. She knows neither of her immediate neighbours beyond courteous nods. This contrasts with her childhood in working class Battersea. Her situation was so very different – poor, but very much part of a community. No doubt there she would have found it impossible to be so decently reclusive as she is now. Her daughter, a single mother struggling to make ends meet, lives up north and she rarely sees her.

Her early experiences are perhaps in part responsible for her inability to strike out of her current depression. At the age of six, in the last war, she was evacuated to Devon. She was one of the unlucky ones – she failed to endear herself to a succession of rural foster parents. Her problem was self-perpetuating; she wet the bed and the more frightened and insecure she became, the more she did so and the more she was shunted from one family to the next. During this time her parents made no effort to see her. Her grandmother visited occasionally – sometimes rescuing her from families where the brutality was too much to ignore.

On her return to London, when she was ten, her parents were like strangers. It is no surprise then that her first love became her husband and he meant everything to her.

In what ways does Greta illustrate the increasing lack of community and aloneness in our society? What would realistically help in her situation? Is there any hope for her, or is she condemned to live and die alone?

2

No longer alone

In 1995, Harold Pinter revived his still very topical twenty-five year old play, *Landscape*, and put it on in London. In it, there are just two elderly characters, a man and a woman, apparently servants in a big house. They sit at a kitchen table throughout the forty minutes of the one-act play. Although they both talk, they do not communicate with each other at all. It is a classic statement of what aloneness means. Pinter has commented bleakly: 'There are two silences. One when no word is spoken. The other when perhaps a torrent of language is employed ... The speech we hear is an indication of what we don't hear. It is a necessary avoidance, a violent, sly, anguished or mocking smokescreen which keeps the other in its place ... One way of looking at speech is to say it is a constant stratagem to cover nakedness.'

The Bible has a word to describe the opposite of 'aloneness,' and the answer to loneliness. It is the Greek word *koinonia*. The word is used fifty-eight times in the New Testament, and means to *share* with someone in something. As is often the case, there is no single English word which expresses the full meaning of the Greek, and *koinonia* is usually translated, depending on the context, as 'fellowship', 'participation' or 'communion.' The related Greek word, *koinonoi* – meaning people who have *koinonia* – has been defined as 'persons who hold property in common; partners or shareholders in a common concern.'[20]

Unfortunately, the most common English translation, 'fellowship,' carries a lot of unnecessary baggage. *Koinonia* has little to do with the subjective camaraderie that people feel with friends or colleagues at the local pub, the Friday morning Mothers and Toddlers' Group or the office party. The fellowship of the Ring in *The Lord of the Rings* is close to the meaning. This company of different races is united in a common purpose – that the Ring of power be destroyed, so that it may no longer enslave. That kind of fellowship requires determination, stamina and courage. In the Bible, *koinonia* is an objective reality that describes someone's status in relation to others, rather than the feelings that person experiences.

There is one New Testament passage that stands out in providing a classic depiction of *koinonia*. In 1 John 1, the word *koinonia* is used four times: twice in verse 3 and in verses 6 and 7. He is writing a general letter, perhaps to a group of churches, at a time when church members were experiencing struggles, conflicts and divisions. What would unite them and mutually strengthen them?

> That which was from the beginning, which we have heard, which we have seen with our eyes, which we have looked at and our hands have touched – this we proclaim concerning the Word of life. The life appeared; we have seen it and testify to it, and we proclaim to you the eternal life, which was with the Father and has appeared to us. We proclaim to you what we have seen and heard, so that you also may have *fellowship* with us. And our *fellowship* is with the Father and with his Son, Jesus Christ. We write this to make our joy complete.

This is the message we have heard from him and declare to you: God is light; in him there is no darkness at all. If we claim to have *fellowship* with him yet walk in the darkness, we lie and do not live by the truth. But if we walk in the light, as he is in the light, we have *fellowship* with one another, and the blood of Jesus, his Son, purifies us from all sin (1 Jn. 1:1-7, emphasis mine).

Notice how the Apostle John uses the word 'fellowship', *koinonia*: 'Our fellowship [*koinonia*] is with the Father and with his Son, Jesus Christ' (verse 4). In other words, John says, ordinary men and women are participating with, sharing with, having something in common with the Father and with the Son. This is an astonishing claim and justifies a closer study of the opening verses of this letter.

John begins in the first two verses by introducing the 'Word of life', a term that sounds very familiar to readers of the New Testament. The 'Word' *is* the Christian message, the Gospel, the good news; it is, as John says, something to be proclaimed. That is why the Bible, the revelation of God, is often called, 'The Word of God', and why Paul urged Timothy to 'Preach the Word'.[21] The Word *is* the message.

But the Christian message is more than just words. According to John, it is the 'Word of life'. In other words, the Christian message has a dynamic; it is a message that brings life; it is a message that changes people.

The most interesting thing of all about John's introduction, however, is that as soon as he puts a name on his message, 'the Word of life', he makes a transition from something that is impersonal to something that is most personal. John says that this message was something he saw with his own eyes and touched with his own hands. This 'Word of life' may be a *message*, but it is also a *person*.

This is not surprising because 'Word' and 'Life' are two of the most common titles for the Lord Jesus Christ. The same Apostle John began his Gospel – the fourth book in the New Testament – by declaring Jesus to be the 'Word of God': 'In the beginning was the Word, and the Word was with God, and the Word was God. He was with God in the beginning.'[22]

Jesus declares himself to be the 'Life.' 'I am the way and the truth and the life. No one comes to the Father except through me.'[23] But Jesus is not just *called* 'Life,' as if it was some abstract, conceptual title: he *is* life. In one of the most profound passages in the Bible, Jesus said, 'A time is coming … when the dead will hear the voice of the Son of God and those who hear will live. For as the Father has life in himself, so he has granted the Son to have life in himself.'[24] It would not be long before Jesus would show what he meant by having 'life in himself.' Having first declared himself to be the 'resurrection and the life',[25] Jesus walked up to the tomb of his friend Lazarus – a man who had been dead for four days – and called out in a loud voice, 'Lazarus, come out!' The Apostle John records what happened next: 'The dead man came out, his hands and feet wrapped with strips of linen, and a cloth around his face.'[26] Jesus is the Word and the Life.

So in his first letter, John insists that the Christian message is not a philosophy and neither is it a message about a person: the message is the person; Christianity *is* Christ. But why proclaim the message? Let John answer: 'We proclaim to you what we have seen and heard, so that you also may have fellowship [*koinonia*] with us. And our fellowship is with the Father and with his Son.'[27] In other words, the end result, the benefit, of hearing the message is to have *koinonia* with God.

In order to grasp the Bible's bold claims about alone-ness and its remedy, it is necessary to take in what the Scriptures teach about God, about humanity and about Christians.

Something about God

Christianity, Islam and Judaism have at least one doctrine in common: there is one God and one God only. The Bible says, 'Hear, O Israel: the Lord our God, the Lord is One.'[28] But the God of Scripture is not solitary. God is One, but God's oneness is a complex unity.

Recall how John in his letter introduces the Lord Jesus Christ as the 'Word of life', as 'that which was from the beginning.' John is telling his readers that right back at the beginning of the Christian story there was a person who could be seen, heard and touched, and John was one of those people who had seen, heard and touched the Lord Jesus Christ. John's language is reminiscent of the opening verses of his Gospel: 'In the beginning was the Word, and the Word was with God'. In other words, Jesus was not only at the beginning of the gospel story, but also before the creation of the world. 'He was with God in the beginning. Through him all things were made; without him nothing was made that has been made.'[29]

So, although God is One, God is not in solitude. There is, within the very nature of God, a dynamic relationship between God the Father and God the Son, the Word. Before time began, God the Father and God the Son enjoyed a relationship of fellowship – of *koinonia*.

It is the unique revelation of New Testament Scripture that God is Oneness and Threeness. That does not mean, however, that the Old Testament contradicts the New

Testament. Indeed, an examination of the Old Testament reveals many clues about the Triune God. Right at the beginning of time, in Genesis 1, the Bible says: 'In the beginning, God created the heavens and the earth.' Although there is nothing in the first verse of the Bible to suggest anything beyond the Oneness of God, the next verse tells us, 'the Spirit of God was hovering over the waters',[30] that is, bringing form out of chaos, and order out of disorder. Still later, as the creation narrative progressively unfolds, God repeatedly speaks in the imperative. He calls, '"Let there be light", and there was light',[31] and then, '"Let there be an expanse…" and it was so.' Seven times God speaks, ushering his creation into existence.

Although the first verse of the Bible introduces the Oneness of God, within half a chapter the Bible asserts that the purposes of God are achieved by the *Spirit of God* and the *Word of God*. Furthermore, when God creates humanity, God the One consults within himself. 'Then God said, "Let *us* make human beings in our image, in our likeness."'[32] In the Bible's first chapter, therefore, God reveals himself as One, but a complex One, in whom there is communication and relationship.

What is the relationship like? Perhaps it is out of order for us to conceive or imagine what God's relationship with himself must be like, and certainly the understanding of men and women will be limited by their finite knowledge and inadequate experience. The New Testament, however, does throw some light onto the very essence and nature of God. In John 17, the Apostle overhears God the Son speaking a prayer to his Father just hours before his arrest and trial. In the prayer, Jesus talks about an arrangement that he has with his Father: God the Father has given his Son authority over all people, that the Son might give eternal life to the people that the Father has given him; the Son, having revealed himself to those people, is now returning to his Father. 'And now Father, glorify me in your presence with the glory I had with you before the world began.'[33] Clearly, the relationship was one of shared decision-making. Jesus also reveals, however, that the relationship is one of love: amongst other things, Jesus prays that his people might one day live with him in heaven and experience the love that the Father and the Son have always enjoyed together.[34]

Something about humanity.

As men and women struggle with their own sense of loneliness, how does a better understanding of God help human beings to understand themselves more completely? Men and women are God's creatures, made in his image, the handiwork of a being that enjoys within his living nature a full and dynamic relationship. This has far-reaching implications: at the heart of the universe there is not solitariness but fellowship, and humans are created to enter and enjoy a love relationship with God.

What was God's assessment of the first man, Adam? 'The Lord God said, "It is not good for the man to be alone."'[35] John Calvin, for one, understood that these words carried a greater significance than a simple reference to marriage. Aloneness is not the will of God either in ordinary life or in the Christian life. Of course it is not: if God is not alone, and the new human being is made in God's image, he or she should not be alone. People need each other as well as needing God.

This need for another is why God created a helper suitable for Adam, who was to be named Eve, and the first-ever human interactions began (for Eve was equally a person). The Garden of Eden was also the first community of the created order. But this community was not a two-way community, just between Adam and Eve; it was a three-way community between Adam, Eve and their Creator. He talked with Adam and Eve, he met the two regularly and he walked in the garden they shared in the cool of the day. Interestingly, the Bible records that Adam and Eve were both naked. The sexual aspect of this statement cannot be denied, of course, but there is a symbol-laden depth to the pronouncement. 'It is a way of saying' Carson reflects, 'that there was no guilt; there was nothing to be ashamed of. This happy innocence meant openness, utter candour. There was nothing to hide, whether from God or from each other.'[36]

It is tragically different one chapter later, when sin has entered into the world! The first consequence of sin is that the man and woman, created by God to enjoy community with God, suffer a loss of community. When God calls to them from within the garden their response is not to run to their Maker and Friend – they both hide in the trees. The relationship, previously characterised by intimacy and joy, has been broken. What is more, the relationship of Adam and Eve with each other, which was also fulfilling and joyful, descends into acrimonious bickering as each blames the other for what has gone wrong. The candour has gone, the innocence has dissipated and the openness has closed.

Today, society offers an enormous range of solutions to men's and women's sense of exclusion, separation and aloneness. Too often, however, people promulgate remedies to the dilemma without agreeing on its cause. The New Age movement advocates tapping into some kind of impersonal being, and sociologists prescribe a plethora of self-help exercises. For its part, however, the Bible insists that at the heart of all human problems – especially mankind's sense of aloneness and exclusion – is rebellion against God, in whose image men and women have been made. Men and women are outside any meaningful relationship with God, and with each other. They are at sea in a storm; they are lost in the ocean's vast spaces, and drift helplessly along without any practical way of getting home.

Something about Christians

What does the Bible's teaching about fellowship say about the Christian? The Christian message is proclaimed, John says, in order that men and women might 'have fellowship with the Father and the Son.' A Christian has fellowship – enjoys *koinonia* – with God. So this Bible word, *koinonia*, is a clearly a very big word, ripe with implication and, in many ways, it describes the highest part of what it means to be Christian. To understand this is important for it is dreadfully possible to embrace Christian values and standards of behaviour, to pursue Christian goals, to cloak oneself with religious customs, to adhere to Christian orthodoxies and to fight for them all, and not to be a Christian at all in the Bible sense of that word. To be a Christian is to 'have fellowship' with God. What does this mean?

First, Christians are *sharers* in God. We have seen the root of the word *koinonia* means to share in something, or to have something in common. So, to have fellowship with God means to share in the life of God, and to be a Christian means nothing less than to share in God's nature. This is the simple message that Christ conveyed when he spoke about the vine. 'I am the vine,' he said to his disciples, 'you are the branches.'[37] What happens to a branch that is not connected to the vine? It withers away and dies. What happens when a branch is connected to the vine? The branch shares the vine's life. Sap flows from the vine into the branch, giving it life, making it part of the vine and enabling it to bear fruit.

The Apostle Peter heard the Lord Jesus Christ in person and it is clear that he grasped the message. Years later he wrote: 'He has given us his very great and precious promises, so that through them you may *participate in the divine nature*.'[38] In other words, a Christian is not someone who has added a little bit of religion or a dose of morality on to their life. Rather they have received divine life. The Apostle Paul talks about this when he says: 'Christ lives in me.'[39] Although the Lord Jesus Christ and the other Bible writers are content to use simple phrases to explain how a Christian shares in the very life of God, the essence of the Christian life – described by Henry Scougal as 'the life of God in the soul of man'[40] – is an unfathomable mystery.

Second, to have fellowship with God means Christians are *partners* with him. The word 'partner' is another root meaning of *koinonia*. What does it mean to be a partner with God? Christians are caught up into God's great purposes and plans for this world and, to the Christian's great delight and surprise, God's interests have become the Christian's interests. God the Father's great enterprise is to send his Son into the world to bring men and women into a personal relationship with himself and to glorify his Son with the glory he had before the world began.[41] But Christians are more than a part of the plan of God the Father, in the sense of a pawn being moved around a chequer board. As partners in God's great enterprise, Christians begin to feel as God feels about things and see as he sees them. Christians do not just see things from a political or economic point of view. They have a completely different view of the world. That is why Christians feel that the good news message, the Gospel, is *their* good news message, and that it is their pleasure and duty to participate with God in a great endeavour to proclaim it to all humanity. And if God grieves and mourns over all kinds of injustice and evil, and all the sad consequences of sin, then the Christian, as God's partner, will likewise grieve and mourn over them.

Third, having fellowship with God means that Christians are *friends* with him. People sometimes talk of sharing something with a friend. Perhaps it is a problem, a secret, an ambition or a dream, but there is great joy in being able to share it with someone else. *Koinonia* carries the same meaning. Adam and Eve hid from God because their friendship with God was broken, and to their great pain, God became a remote stranger, no longer a friend.

Fourth, for Christians to have fellowship with God means that they are his *children*. Here, the Apostle John takes his readers even deeper into the meaning of *koinonia*. 'Our fellowship is with the Father'.[42] Consider the astonishing implications of John's statement. The Christian is someone who turns to God, the Maker of heaven and earth, the One who sustains all things by the power of his Word, the almighty, sovereign, unchanging Being, and says, 'Father!'

He is not, by right, everybody's Father. John said, 'Yet to all who received him, to those who believed in his name, he gave the right to become children of God – children born not of natural descent, nor of human decision or a husband's will, but born of God.'[43]

Paul, writing to the church established in Rome, spoke of the Spirit of adoption, by whom Christians cry 'Abba, Father,'[44] and the Apostle John, later in his first letter, wrote: 'We know that we live in him and he in us, because he has given us of his Spirit.'[45]

There is a story of a couple who had two children. After the birth of a son, the woman was unable to bear more children, so the couple decided to adopt a baby girl. Years later the man would introduce acquaintances to his family with, 'Please meet my son,' and then, with a broad grin and a proud huff he would pronounce, 'and this is my *chosen* daughter.'

God has only one Son, the Lord Jesus Christ, who is eternally begotten of the Father. But God the Father has countless thousands of adopted children, and he is to each of them, the same that he is to his eternal Son – a proud Father. For the Christian, then, God is no longer a stranger, a stray power, an extraterrestrial force or a cosmic energy. The Apostle Paul talks about Christians like this: 'Formerly, when you did not know God, you were slaves ... But now you know God – or rather are known by God'.[46] In other words, the Christian knows him and he in turn knows the Christian. This is God's community; a community that is genuine, where relationships are intimate and where friendships are reciprocal.

Paul eulogises: 'Oh, the depths of the riches of the wisdom and knowledge of God! How unsearchable his judgements, and his paths beyond tracing out! ... To him be the glory for ever! Amen.'[47]

Cathryn: Isolation despite appearances

Cathryn is a single woman in her late thirties who lives alone with her two cats. As a partner in a solicitors' practice, she works six days a week and socialises with friends over dinner and at bridge. To all intents and purposes, she seems very busy and sociable. Yet, when you look deeper, it transpires she has built a self-protective wall around herself, following traumatic experiences in her mid-twenties. After being married for only a short time, she became seriously ill. Her husband could not cope with the experience and they quickly divorced. Having lost her husband and nearly her life, she understandably developed strong self-reliance to ensure she could never be hurt in this way again. She is now open with very few people, believing that it is safer to play your cards close to your chest.

Do John's opening words in his letter offer any substantial help for Cathryn? What is there in these verses that might get past her barriers?

3

Lost in space

It is already apparent that the Bible has a great deal to say about our human sense of separation and aloneness. God made men and women in his image, and just as God is not alone – he enjoys fellowship within himself – so God created men and women to enjoy community with their Maker and with each other. Aloneness and loneliness are not part of God's will for humanity, and especially not for Christian people.

We saw that here is one word that sums up the Bible's answer to loneliness: the Greek word *koinonia*, translated by the English word 'fellowship', and meaning to share with someone in something. Adam and Eve lost their *koinonia* with God. When sin had entered, instead of running *to* God when he called them from the Garden, they ran *from* God, the relationship broken. The Christian is different: the Christian is someone who has heard God's call and has run *back to* God, the friendship and relationship restored. So when the Apostle John wrote his first letter and described Christian people as those who enjoy *koinonia* with God and with each other, he did not use the word *koinonia* in a subjective, fuzzy sense. For John, the very essence of the Christian life is about relationship.

There is, however, a second important aspect of *koinonia* which goes beyond the relationship of men and women with God. Just as Adam and Eve, having lost relationship with God, then began to suffer loss of community with each other, so also Christians, once their relationship with their Maker has been restored have, in John's words, 'fellowship with one another.'[48] This second aspect of *koinonia* must wait until later chapters but for now, the Apostle John has more to say about the Christian's relationship with God. God is a Trinity, God in three persons, and the Christian enjoys a relationship with each member of the Godhead.

The Christian's relationship with God the Father

In his great prayer, just hours before his arrest and trial, Jesus explained what it was to be a Christian, describing eternal life in terms of relationship. 'Now this is eternal life: that they may know you, the only true God, and Jesus Christ, whom you have sent.'[49] There is a deliberate order in Jesus' words: he does not talk about knowing the Son and, then, about knowing the only true God that sent the Son. Relationship with God begins with God the Father.

In the same way, when the Apostle John writes about relationship, his foremost thought is the Christian's relationship with God the Father. 'Our fellowship is with the Father,' he says and, later, 'whoever acknowledges the Son has the Father also.'[50] For John, to *acknowledge* the Son is to *have*, or possess, the Father. In other words, when anybody comes to see for themselves that Jesus Christ is the unique, eternal Son of the Living God, and acknowledges the same, and bows their knee to his lordship over their lives, then, and by virtue of that acknowledgement, that person is given a relationship with God the Father.

It is the unique revelation of Scripture that God the Father is jealous for his Son's glory. Indeed, such is his great desire for the honour of his Son that, when men and women put their confidence and trust in him, God the Father adopts them into his family: he becomes their Father and they become his children. The Apostle John said the same in the first chapter of his gospel: 'Yet to all who received him, to those who believed in his name, he [the Father] gave the right to become children of God.'[51] No one enters God's family by virtue of their race, or their birth in a 'Christian' country. There is only one way to become a child of God: by adoption.

The Christian's relationship with God the Son

The Apostle John, in his first letter, has already described the Christian life as having fellowship with the Father and with his Son. The Christian, who bears the name of Christ and who is a follower of Christ, has fellowship with Christ. In John's second letter, he adds, 'Anyone who runs ahead and does not continue in the teaching of Christ does not have God; whoever continues in the teaching has both the Father and the Son.'[52] John did not originate this teaching, for Jesus himself had said: 'Those who love me will obey my teaching. My Father will love them, and we will come to them and make our home with them.'[53]

This is one of the most overlooked, undervalued, under-quoted and most wonderful promises of Holy Scripture: God 'makes his home' with ordinary Christian men and women. The original Greek words carry inti-

macy and familiarity. These are the same words that
people would use to describe their best friends coming
round for an evening, sitting in the best armchair, kick-
ing off their shoes and helping themselves to a beer from
the fridge. God is the King of all Kings and the Lord of
all Lords. There is no one more important and no one
more regal, yet he promises to make his home with his
people. Here is what the Apostle John teaches about
Christians that have 'Jesus at home.'

First, Christians have Jesus's *salvation*. This is one of
the great themes of John's first letter. 'This is love: not
that we loved God, but that he loved us and sent his Son
as an atoning sacrifice for our sins.'[54] Unfortunately,
'atoning sacrifice' is not the best translation of the Greek
word, *hilasterion*. The footnote in most New International
Versions provides a better explanation: 'As the one who
would turn aside his wrath.'

Most of John's original readers would have understood exactly what John was saying. Under the Old
Covenantal system, God had prescribed numerous
animal sacrifices with different preparatory rituals, cul-
minating in a series of elaborate ceremonies on the Day
of Atonement. The sacrifices, however, shared one thing
in common: the sacrificed animals were all innocent
victims. Whenever the Bible talks about an atoning sacrifice, the thought is of a mysterious transaction, where
justified wrath is turned aside from a *guilty* offender
onto an *innocent* substitute. Some older Bible translations
use the English word 'propitiation.' An atoning sacrifice
propitiates God's anger, turning it away from the guilty
onto the innocent. This notion is uppermost when God
commanded the High Priest, Aaron, to 'lay both hands
on the head of the live goat and confess over it all the
wickedness and rebellion of the Israelites – all their sins
– and put them on the goat's head.'[55]

The Bible is a progressive record of God's revelation, and thus the New Testament provides a retrospective commentary on the Old Testament. The New Testament makes it plain that the thousands of Old Covenant sacrifices were, in themselves, ineffective in this most important respect: 'It is impossible for the blood of bulls and goats to take away sins.'[56] So if the sacrificial system was unable to deal with the Israelites' core problems, why did God ordain it? Again, the New Testament is clear: each sacrifice, repeated 'endlessly year after year',[57] continually taught the people of Israel vital truths about the God of heaven and earth: God is holy, he takes sin seriously and the penalty of sin can only be paid with an atoning sacrifice. In this way, therefore, the sacrifice of countless lambs and goats pointed to a sacrifice that *was* able to propitiate God's anger. John the Baptist had understood these truths. When Jesus came to John the Baptist for baptism, John immediately recognised that God's atoning sacrifice was not an animal, but a person. 'Look,' John cried out, 'the Lamb of God, who takes away the sin of the world!'[58]

This is the heart of the Christian message of good news. Christians know that the very last drop of the wrath of God that they deserve has been deflected away and diverted onto the Lamb of God hanging upon the cross. There are only two categories of people: those who are still waiting for the wrath of God to fall upon them, and those who know that God's wrath has already fallen – has already been exhausted, or propitiated – in the person of the Lord Jesus Christ on the cross. It is this latter category of people – countless thousands of men and women – who can heartily sing the words of the old hymn: –

Because my sinless Saviour died,
My guilty soul is counted free.

For God the just was satisfied,
To look at him and pardon me.

Secondly, to 'have Jesus at home' means to *share in his life*. 'This is how God showed his love among us: he sent his one and only Son into the world so that we might live through him.'[59] The Christian is the person who receives eternal life in place of certain death.

There is a day coming for all people when they will breathe their last breath, and slip through death into eternity. For Christians, there is nothing more wonderful than the knowledge that they will open their eyes in the presence of the Lord Jesus Christ. On the contrary, there is nothing more miserable than the death of those who die without Christ and without hope. The humanist and secular philosopher may reduce the Christian message into an insipid, wishy-washy creed or a code of behaviour, but at eternity's door, the real reason why Christ came into the world is drawn into the sharpest focus: 'that we might live through him.'

The Christian's relationship with God the Spirit

The Christian's relationship with God is not limited to God the Father and God the Son: the Christian also has a relationship with God the Spirit. In his first letter, John writes, 'We know that we live in him and he in us, because he has given us of his Spirit.'[60]

In Acts 2, when the Apostle Peter preaches the first Christian sermon to the huge crowds that gathered on the Day of Pentecost, he concludes with two appeals: 'Repent and be baptised, every one of you, in the name of Jesus Christ.'[61] The first appeal was internal: Peter urges repentance which, in the proper biblical sense, means to turn away, deep down inside the heart, from wrong actions and from wrong views about Jesus. Up to that time, Peter's hearers had been thinking that Jesus was a failed carpenter from Galilee, a dead-and-buried no-hoper. But Peter shows them, principally from the Old Testament Scriptures, that they are wrong in their thinking about Jesus and he insists that the gathered crowds must turn around and think of Jesus as God's anointed Messiah. 'Therefore let all Israel be assured of this: God has made this Jesus, whom you crucified, both Lord and Christ.'[62] Peter's second appeal was external: he commands them to be baptised, 'in the name of Jesus Christ' as a public demonstration that Jesus Christ had become their Saviour also.

Having given two appeals, however, Peter immediately goes on to offer two gifts: the gift of forgiveness and the gift of the Spirit.[63] The giving of the Spirit is the birthright of every believer. That is why the Apostle Paul can say that 'if anyone does not have the Spirit of Christ, that person does not belong to Christ.'[64] The Spirit is the greatest gift of the ascended Christ to his church on earth. This is not a surprise since the Holy Spirit is the source of all the other gifts and graces that Christians need to live as God's children in the world. The Spirit has a role in assuring Christians that they have eternal life – 'this is how we know he lives in us: we know it by the Spirit he gave us.'[65] He has a role in leading Christian people into an understanding of the truth: 'you have an anointing from the Holy One, and all of you know the truth.'[66] It is the Holy Spirit who produces the love of God in Christian men and women for other men and women. God is love, and wherever his Spirit is active, the evidence will be seen in love. But the most prominent role of the Spirit is to unite the Christian with God.

Of course, there are many other religions that talk about union with God, particularly the Eastern religions and the New Age movement. For these religions, the notion of union with the divine means that adherents lose their identities and becomes submerged in a kind of cosmic consciousness. But the Bible's concept of union with God is different: the Christian's individuality and identity will be retained. On the last day, the Day of Resurrection, the Christian will be changed, the perishable will be raised imperishable, the mortal will be clothed with immortality, but the Christian will not lose his or her identity. Christian men and women will be made more human, not less, made more like Jesus Christ, not less, and made more like God had originally made men and women to be. People, however, will be able to recognise individual Christians, just as Jesus' disciples were able to recognise Jesus after he had been resurrected.

This concept of union with God is behind the Apostle Paul's repeated expression, 'in Christ.' The Christian believer shares in each aspect of Christ's redemptive work: the Christian has died with Christ, has been raised with him, presently reigns with him, and one day that same Christian will share Christ's glory.[67]

What does this say about the Christian? The foundations of the universe may fall apart, but nothing can ever sever the connection between God and his people. The Christian's salvation is unshakeable, unassailable and as secure as the very life of God is secure. This is what Augustus Toplady had to say about Christian security: –

My name, from the palms of His hands
Eternity will not erase
Engraved on His heart it remains
In marks of indelible grace.

Yes, I to the end shall endure
As sure as the earnest is given
More happy, but not more secure,
the glorified spirits in Heaven[68]

In other words, Christians glorified in heaven may be happier than those that remain on this side of eternity, but their salvation is not more complete. 'Who shall separate us from the love of Christ?' asked the Apostle Paul. 'Shall trouble or hardship or persecution or famine or nakedness or danger or sword?' Listen to Paul triumphantly answer his own question: 'No, in all these things we are more than conquerors through him who loved us.'[69]

* * * *

One of the obvious features that jump off the pages of John's first letter is the writer's pastoral heart and evident concern for his readers. John knew that although there was nothing that could end the Christian's relationship with God, there were, nonetheless, things that could spoil their relationship with God. Again, let John explain:

This is the message we have heard from him and declare to you: God is light; in him there is no darkness at all. If we claim to have fellowship with him yet walk in the darkness, we lie and do not live by the truth. But if we walk in the light, as he is in the light, we have fellowship with one another, and the blood of Jesus, his Son, purifies us from all sin.

If we claim to be without sin, we deceive ourselves and the truth is not in us. If we confess our sins, he is faithful and just and will forgive us our sins and purify us from all unrighteousness. If we claim we have not sinned, we make him out to be a liar and his word has no place in our lives (I Jn. 1:5-10).

Although a human father's love for his children is, at best, a shadow of God's eternal love for his adopted children, some similarities can be drawn. A human father may speak of the pain that has been caused by a rebellious and wayward son, yet even the hardest of fathers would recognise that his son was still his son. The relationship may be spoiled, but it has not ended. Similarly, there are things that can spoil the Christian's relationship with his Father. John makes this clear by reminding his readers about God's character: God is light. The person that Christians enjoy a relationship with, John insists, is full of truth and purity.

The first thing that can spoil the Christian's relationship with God is *wrong belief* Look carefully at how John successively deals with three false claims: 'If we claim to have fellowship with him yet walk in the darkness, we lie,' (6); 'If we claim to be without sin, we deceive ourselves' (8); and finally, 'If we claim to have not sinned, we make him out to be a liar' (10). One after the other, John hits areas of wrong belief. Today, the same areas of wrong belief abound wherever and whenever people want fellowship with God on easy terms. There is however no alternative to divine revelation: either people believe what God has said in the Bible or they opt for the darkness of their own human speculation.

Secondly, *wrong behaviour* can spoil the Christian's relationship with God. For the New Testament writers, wrong behaviour follows from wrong belief, and bad behaviour comes between the Christian and God. John writes: 'Do not love the world or anything in the world.

If you love the world, the love of the Father is not in you. For everything in the world – the cravings of sinful people, the lust of their eyes and the boasting of what they have and do – comes not from the Father but from the world. The world and its desires pass away, but whoever does the will of God lives for ever.'[70] Again: 'This is how we know who the children of God are and who the children of the devil are: Those who do not do what is right are not God's children; nor are those who do not love their brothers and sisters.'[71]

John is teaching that Christians cannot expect an unblemished relationship with their heavenly Father if they refuse to repent from sinful, rebellious actions or, for example, from an adulterous relationship. Indeed, the lesson of Scripture is that when the Christian's relationship with God deteriorates, then likewise, their relationship with other Christians will also deteriorate. People who profess to love God, then fail to love God's people, have not understood the full impact of this Bible word, *koinonia*.

* * * *

The Apostle John goes beyond teaching his readers how the Christian's relationship with God cannot be *ended* and how the Christian's relationship can be *spoiled*: he also teaches Christians how to *maintain* the relationship. 'Walk in the light, as he is in the light.' John is saying that the Christians should bring their thinking and actions out into the open and place them under the searchlight of God's truth – his self-revelation in Scripture. This is why Christian people read the Scriptures for themselves and worship at churches where the Bible is proclaimed Sunday after Sunday. To walk in the light means that Christians will put themselves in a place where God can speak to them and deal with their sins. There are risks whenever Christians expose themselves to the light of God's truth and, for many, it is an uncomfortable experience. Sometimes, it is an easier option is to attend a church where the challenge is less.

It is the common experience of many Christians who sit under a regular Bible-teaching ministry that they feel prodded and poked. Perhaps they thought they were 'nice' people and now they discover that there are areas of their lives that are full of bitterness and anger. Perhaps they conclude they are not very 'nice' people at all, or perhaps they blame the preacher! As God's Word is preached, however, it is God the Holy Spirit who does the prodding and poking at people's lives. As the Christian walks in the light, the Spirit surgically snips away, pulling apart the pieces, and uncovering things the Christian had never experienced before. Bible-based, preaching ministries should carry a Health Warning: 'Beware! No one can sit under this ministry for long without suffering an unexplained crisis of the mind, heart or life!'

There are two challenges that many Christians must confront if they are to walk in the light: there are some areas about which they will not let God speak to them, and there are some people through whom they will not let God speak to them. For the Christian, 'walking in the light' means that previously obscured things must come out into the open. It is nearly every Christian's normal experience that depths of sin and deceit emerge from their heart, often when they thought that they had mastered such sins. Sometimes a Christian may experience sordid desires, such as an addiction to sex, or sometimes the Christian may experience sinful attitudes, such as a destructive desire for recognition.

What is the Christian to do? Sin, in all its forms, must be confronted and teased out from the shadows into

God's searching light of God. Psychologists talk of the power of 'denial.' A smoker may tell herself that one more cigarette won't do any harm; a dieter may say that one more piece of chocolate won't make any difference and a drunk-driver may convince himself that he is a better driver if he has 'one for the road.' All these, however, are examples of cognitive distortions, where smokers, dieters or even drunk-drivers are giving themselves permission to indulge their craving or desire. To the psychologist, a cognitive distortion throws a cloak over reality.

It is the same for the Christian in relationship to God. 'Walk in the light as he is in the light.' There is no cloak large enough to hide a single sin from God. God knows what Christians think about their fellow Christians, what web sites they have been browsing, and what television programmes they have watched. But the Christian is not to hide from God, as Adam and Eve did. Rather Christians are to confess to God what they have discovered about themselves and thankfully they are to lay hold of the provision God has made in Jesus for cleansing. 'If we confess our sins, he is faithful and just and will forgive us our sins and purify us from all unrighteousness.'[72] Thus the Apostle John urges the Christian to keep short accounts with God, confessing our sins each day and dealing with sin as it arises.

This behaviour is unnatural for every member of the human race. A child, for example, breaks a vase, and his parents return home to find fifty smashed pieces of pottery all over the kitchen floor. The parents might ask: 'Do you know what happened to that vase?' How often does the child reply, 'What vase?' Ever since Adam and Eve's first sin, our instinct is to deny the sin, rather than confess it. Christians, however, enjoy freedom from fear in their relationship with God, as it is built upon regular and consistent openness.

The Bible's answer to synthetic Christianity is to be 'out in the open' with God. Reality is the opposite of denial, and 'real' Christians are less likely to be critical and judgemental about other men and women. On the contrary, those who do not have an open and frank relationship with God are most likely to be proud and superior in their attitudes towards others, especially towards those who have failed.

Bill and June: Transient communities, case 1

The world is a smaller place. Previous generations lived and died within the same village. Today, it is a very real chance that your grown-up child will marry an antipodean and emigrate.

Bill and June, Essex born and bred, are well into their forties and have two children, newly graduated and at the beginning of their careers. The parents would like to plan for the future, thinking ahead to retirement and where they might live. They find themselves held to ransom, however, as they conclude that wherever their children end up, they want to live close to at least one of them. The children, however, are a long way from putting down roots themselves. The situation begins to verge on the ridiculous as Bill and June speculate on the possible outcome of their daughter's very new relationship with a Geordie she met at university. Do they really want to head that far north?

Humour aside, this scenario presents a very real conundrum for parents with grown-up children. (The situation becomes even more complex if the parents' marriage has failed.) Our lives can consist of temporary membership of a succession of communities, as life's path takes us from one place to the next. In our prime, this can be exciting and invigorating, but later in life it can lead to tremendous loneliness as we find ourselves living amongst a community we do not really know.

Is there any consolation for Bill and June in the fact that we can share in the fellowship with God that John talks about? Can this reality help them in their decision-making at one of the crisis points of life? How might it help the way they think about their children?

4

Love changes everything

In their 1992 song *Everybody Hurts*, the highly successful rock band R.E.M. tackled the issue of suicide in young men. It is an anthem for our times, highlighting loneliness as the thing that drives people to the verge of despair. Others are less sympathetic, attributing the mounting suicide rates to young people's inability to socialise.

Irrespective of how sympathetic people are to the problems facing youngsters in Western society, everyone recognises that suicide rates will never reduce without a greater sense of community. Deep down in the human psyche, men and women, young and old, are searching for a sense of belonging, togetherness and identity. Many popular films, songs and television programmes owe their success to their ability, often unintentionally, to touch a chord with these needs. One such endearing television show is *Cheers*, first screened in 1982. Ted Danson plays Sam Malone, the owner of the 'Cheers' bar in Boston, Massachusetts. In Sam's bar, life is portrayed as a series of regular, random encounters with friends. There are spats, rivalries and grievances but they are heard in short order and any tensions are quickly resolved. Like the young men considering suicide in the

R.E.M. song, the men and women in Sam Malone's bar want community.

People want love. Woody Allen acknowledged that, for screenplays at least, love makes the world go around. He said that all his films, 'deal with that greatest of all difficulties – love relationships. Everybody encounters that. People are either in love, about to fall in love, on the way out of love, looking for love, or a way to avoid it'.[73]

The musical *Aspects of Love*, written by Andrew Lloyd-Webber, opened on Broadway in April 1990. It is based on a true story – the autobiography of David Garnett, the nephew of Virginia Woolf – and begins with a seventeen-year-old man called Alex who falls in love with Rose Vibert, a twenty-five-year old actress from a touring theatre. In the show's most famous song, the young Alex celebrates his new-found, if not painful love. He sings of love changing everything, bringing you glory and bringing you shame. He concludes that nothing in the world after falling in love will ever be the same.

Ultimately, men and women's search for community is a search for love. Mother Teresa worked in the slums of Calcutta amongst thousands of people who lacked the most basic needs such as food, elementary healthcare and sanitary conditions. After travelling to Britain, America and Australia, however, she wrote, 'People today are hungry for love, for understanding-love which is … the only answer to loneliness and great poverty.'[74]

* * * *

The Bible has much to say about love and loving communities. Jesus said, 'a new commandment I give you: Love one another. As I have loved you, so you must love one another. By this everyone will know that you are my disciples, if you love one another.'[75] The Apostle Paul exhorted the early Christian men and women to 'be devoted to one another with mutual affection.'[76]

The Apostle John, however, gives Christian people some of the most comprehensive teaching about community. He does this by using *koinonia*, this big Bible word we have been exploring, to link fellowship with God and fellowship within communities. Through the proclamation of the gospel message, God brings men and women into a full, real, joyful relationship with himself. The second aspect to *koinonia* is full, real, joyful relationship with other Christian men and women. John wanted his readers to experience joy in the gospel *message* and in the gospel *community*. 'We write this,' he insisted right at the beginning of his first letter, 'to make your joy complete.'[77]

In John's mind, *koinonia* and love were two sides to the same coin: without love, there is no fellowship, and there can be no genuine gospel community, without love. In 1 John 4, he exhorts:

Dear friends, let us love one another, for love comes from God. Everyone who loves has been born of God and knows God. Whoever does not love does not know God, because God is love. This is how God showed his love among us: He sent his one and only Son into the world that we might live through him. This is love: not that we loved God, but that he loved us and sent his Son as an atoning sacrifice for our sins. Dear friends, since God so loved us, we also ought to love one another. No one has ever seen God; but if we love one another, God lives in us and his love is made complete in us.

We know that we live in him and he in us, because he has given us of his Spirit. And we have seen and testify that the Father has sent his Son to be the Saviour of the world. If any acknowledge that Jesus is the Son of God, God lives in them and they in God. And so we know and rely on the love God has for us.

God is love. Those who live in love live in God, and God in them. In this way, love is made complete among us so that we will have confidence on the day of judgement, because in this world we are like him. There is no fear in love. But perfect love drives out fear, because fear has to do with punishment. The one who fears is not made perfect in love.

We love because he first loved us. If we say we love God yet hate a brother or sister, we are liars. For any of us who do not love a brother or sister, whom we have seen, cannot love God, whom we have not seen. And he has given us this command: Those who love God must also love one another (1 Jn. 4: 7-21).

In this passage, John's repeated exhortation to 'love one another,' is passionate and unmistakable, and is based on three reasons: God's nature, his gift and his present activity.

God's nature

John shapes his first argument for mutual love by reminding his readers about God's nature. He uses two slightly differing expressions. First, 'love comes from God',[78] and second, 'God is love.'[79] The first expression teaches that God is the source of all love. This stands to reason: God is the Creator of the universe and therefore of every good thing in the universe, especially love. Because God is the fount from which all love flows, then anyone who loves, must love with that love which comes from God and, therefore, they must be born of God.

John's little book, often described as 'the tests of life',[80] stands out as a stark challenge to all professing Christians. Can someone ever have any proof that they have been born again? John insists they can. He gives the test of *doctrine*: what someone believes about the Lord Jesus Christ. Then John gives the test of *morality*: how someone is behaving. Lastly, he gives the test of *love*: how someone responds to other Christians. Everyone who has been born again of the Spirit of God will love other Christians because 'everyone who loves has been born of God.' In Bible terms, a Christian that does not love other Christians represents an oxymoron.

John's second expression about God's nature is even more profound: 'God is love.' Love, John says, is far more than an *aspect* of God: any examination of the depths of God's nature will reveal love. Whatever else there is to state about God would be inadequate, incomplete, and in error, without saying that God is love. This simple and profound statement stands with a trilogy of Bible revelations that John names about the essence of God: God is Spirit;[81] (he isn't physical and material); God is light;[82] (he is transparently holy, without any dark folds or hidden agendas); and God is love.

John emphasises the divine nature of love by linking love to each of the members of the Trinity. In 1 John 4, verses 7 and 8, his reference is to God the Father. In verses 9 to 11 his reference is to God the Son, and then in verse 12, the phrase 'God lives in us' is a reference to God the Holy Spirit. God the Father is love, God the Son is love, and God the Holy Spirit is love. There is no part of the nature of God that is not permeated with love.

This is a unique Christian revelation: no Greek, Roman, Egyptian, or Babylonian in Christ's day, or in the centuries before him, had ever conceived that the heart of God is love. This reality is also a great motivator for

Christian people. Christians cannot always explain injustice, suffering, and pain, but they are comforted when they recall that the core of God's being is love. Christians often finds mission difficult and discouraging, but are stirred to renew their labours in the certain knowledge that God has a great love for lost men and women. Most of all, when Christians find it difficult to get on with other Christians – let alone to love them – they are spurred on by John's words, 'let us love one another, for love comes from God.'[83]

God's gift

Christians are also to love one another, John says, because God has given his Son.[84] When John uses phrases such as 'born of God', and 'that we might live through him', he is highlighting the initiative that God has made. God gave his Son when people were spiritually lifeless. We do not take this Bible teaching seriously enough. The Apostle Paul said, 'As for you, you were dead in your transgressions and sins ... But because of his great love for us, God, who is rich in mercy, made us alive with Christ.'[85] Those who are dead towards God are unable to respond to him, make any positive moral step towards him, or love him. They are spiritually dead and their greatest need is that the power of God should enter their souls and revitalise them. Jesus said, 'I tell you the truth, a time is coming and has now come when the dead will hear the voice of the Son of God and those who hear will live.'[86] The truth of Jesus' words was demonstrated later when he walked up to Lazarus' tomb and commanded a man who had been dead and rotting for four days to come out. There is life in the voice of the Son of God. Lazarus did not contribute to the miracle and neither did he exercise any initiative. It is the same when anyone becomes a Christian. Men and women are dead, spiritually dead towards God, and there is no hope unless the power of God resuscitates them.

What is God's love-gift?

'This is how God showed his love among us: He sent his one and only Son into the world that we might live through him.'[87] There is no more precious gift. If a natural father cannot comprehend of anything more precious than his children, who can comprehend anything more precious to God than his Son, Jesus Christ? God is the Creator and Sustainer of the universe: if it pleased God, he could have merely spoken, created a completely new galaxy of planets and stars, filled its planets with gold, diamonds, and other precious gems, and given it to men and women. It would be a wonderful gift – rather like a millionaire emptying his wallet and giving it to a street beggar. But God could create a replacement galaxy as easily as the millionaire could refill his wallet.

The gift that John speaks of, however, could never be replaced. God's Son wasn't created; he eternally proceeds from the Father. In addition, Jesus was not one son out of many: he is God's one and *only* Son. This is why the Bible calls Jesus, 'God's indescribable gift.'[88]

Why did God send his love-gift?

If Jesus had come into this world, coming down to human size and putting on our skin, breathing our air, to be a teacher, then that would have been wonderful, and more than human beings deserve. If Jesus had come into the world to show men and women how to behave, then that also would have been wonderful. God, however, did not send his Son as a teacher or as a moral crusader: he 'sent his Son as an atoning sacrifice for our sins.'[89] This stark, simple fact captures the heart of every believer, who says with the Apostle Paul, 'the Son of God … loved me and gave himself for me.'[90]

The meaning behind 'atoning sacrifice' was introduced in the last chapter but for now, notice how the Apostle John borrows his language from the story of God testing Abraham.[91] All Abraham and Sarah had ever wanted was their own child. Year after year, they had waited, until Sarah had passed the menopause and was barren. Then finally, as God had promised, Isaac was born and he became the apple of his father's eye. Then God came to Abraham and asked him to sacrifice his son, his only son, Isaac, whom he loved. To Abraham's credit, he was prepared to do what God said: he took Isaac to the place of the sacrifice and told him to gather wood. Isaac was puzzled, asking his father: 'The fire and the wood are here … but where is the lamb for the burnt offering?' Abraham bound Isaac and, believing that God must be able to bring him back from the dead, raised his knife to plunge it deep into his son's heart. At that moment, God stopped Abraham and spared Isaac by providing a substitute sacrifice.

There was no such escape for God's Son. God 'did not spare his own Son, but gave him up for us all.'[92] God sent his only Son into a hostile environment, into a rebel world, on a rescue mission to redeem sinful men and women and reconcile them to God. God could not provide a substitute sacrifice for Jesus, as he had done for Isaac, because Jesus was the substitute sacrifice.

John has already given two reasons that stir Christians to 'love one another.' If Christians share anything of God's nature, then they should love one another and also, if Christians understand anything of God's gift, then they should love one another. But there is a third reason.

God's present activity

God's love is not only seen in his eternal nature, and in the historical accomplishments of Jesus on the cross. At this moment, God is at work in the world through his people. John tells us, 'No one has ever seen God; but if we love each other, God lives in us and his love is made complete in us.'[93]

It is plain that no one has seen God. There are several occasions in the Old Testament where God revealed his glory. He revealed his splendour to Isaiah in the Temple. 'I saw the Lord seated on a throne, high and exalted, and the train of his robe filled the Temple.'[94] Ezekiel also saw visions of God's glory, and he wrote them down using extraordinary apocalyptical language.[95] Moses, when he had led the people of Israel out of Egypt, asked God to show him his glory. God agreed. He put Moses in the cleft of a rock and passed by him. God, however, did not permit Moses to see his face, explaining that 'no one may see me and live.'[96] The Old Testament visions were not appearances; they were revelations – God communicating himself to the prophets at a level that they could grasp. So how is a person ever going to see God today? The answer is breathtaking. Though God cannot be seen in himself, he can be seen in those in whom he lives. The invisible God becomes visible when Christian people love each other.

* * * *

John has drawn together three arguments – God's nature, God's gift and God's present activity – and he draws his conclusion with a powerful exhortation: 'Dear friends, since God so loved us, we also ought to love one another.'[97] Since God is love, all our definitions of what love is and how love behaves must be drawn from him. The love, which is the proof of a true relationship with God, is a love that acts for the benefit of others even at risk to itself, even to the point of costly self-sacrifice. It is a practical love. 'Dear children', says John, 'Let us not love with words or tongue but with actions and in truth.'[98] One of the surest means of promoting love is to act in a loving manner. God's love for men and women is not mere words. He was not content to say he loved men and women; God *shows* his love for men and women. The great challenge that Christian people face today is to stop telling God that they love him, and start showing him that they love him. Christian love is love in action, and is the final apologetic or convincing proof for a watching world.

This highlights the importance of *koinonia* in contemporary Western Society. If Christians are going to make an impact in a society of fragmented families and broken relationships, people must be able to look at gospel communities and see Christians loving one another. Society is filled with people who, feeling lonely and isolated, are searching for love and community. There is nothing more attractive than a community filled with love. This is not a sociological argument: it is Christ's argument. 'By this shall everyone know that you are my disciples, if you love one another.' The pagan world looked at the early Christian movement and said, 'see how they love one another.'[99] Such loving *koinonia* remains a compelling magnet for people who are not yet Christians.

How are Christians to love one another? Jesus said, 'love each other as I have loved you.'[100] The normal characteristic of human love is to love those who deserve it. Everyone finds it easy to love people that they 'get on with', 'click with', or those who will love them back. Jesus had a blistering word to say to those who love like that. 'If you love those who love you, what reward will you get? Are not even the tax collectors doing that? And if you greet only your own people, what are you doing more than others? Do not even the pagans do that?'[101] Jesus is not impressed with this kind of love; anyone can love like that. No one needs the life of God to flow into their soul in order to love other people as the world loves them. Christian love demands a supernatural explanation.

The Greeks had several words for standard love, including *eros*. *Eros* describes love between equals – love where there is mutual attraction or love among those who like each other. God is the source of all such love, and it is wonderful thing. Such love helps like-minded people to get on, it is the basis for friendships and it fires up romance. It is not, however, exclusive to Christianity – the tax collectors and pagans have this standard love.

The early Christian writers took a hitherto rarely used Greek word and immersed it with Christian ideas. It is the Greek word, *agape*, the Bible's favourite word to describe Christian love. *Agape* is exclusive to Christian people. It is a self-giving, sacrificial love without attached conditions. Most human love is conditional. 'I'll love you, if you love me. I'll be faithful, if you're faithful.' *Agape* is different. It cuts across the world's value systems and embraces those for whom the world has no time. It stretches across barriers of prejudice to touch people the world does not like. The religious leaders in Jesus' day could not understand why Jesus touched lepers and associated with prostitutes and the no-hopers. Today, the world still cannot understand *agape*. But it does get the world's attention.

It is this love, then, that is the basis of *koinonia*. Later chapters will work out in practical detail what it means to love like this. The Apostle John, however, gives the starting point: 'We love because he first loved us.'[102] In the next verse, John argues that because other human beings are visible, it is easier to love them than God, who is not visible. Therefore, if love for people is absent, then love for God is also absent. The reverse is also true: to love other people is to love God. John makes a simple, stunning conclusion: 'He has given us this command: Those who love God must also love one another.'[103] Christians learn to love the invisible God by loving the visible community of God's people.

The greatest mark of the church is love. Paul, when writing to the young Christian church at Corinth, categorised the Christian life under three great, abiding virtues of faith, hope and love and concluded by saying that, 'the greatest of these is love.'[104] Read how the Apostle cannot define Christian love without showing it in action.

> Love is patient, love is kind. It does not envy, it does not boast, it is not proud. It is not rude, it is not self-seeking, it is not easily angered, it keeps no record of wrongs. Love does not delight in evil but rejoices with the truth. It always protects, always trusts, always hopes, always perseveres. Love never fails.[105]

Love is the pre-eminent Christian virtue. If one were to successively remove love from every other Christian virtue, the product would be sub-Christian. To remove love from joy would result in hedonism and selfish pleasure seeking. To remove love from holiness would result in self-righteousness, imposing rules and regulations with a judgemental and over-critical spirit. To remove love from truth would result in cold, bitter orthodoxy, where people believe the right things but in the wrong spirit. To remove love from mission would result in imperialism, where churches despatch armies and baptise the masses at the point of a sword. To remove love from unity would result in boring unifor- mity, where everyone is obliged to conform to someone else's ideas and plans.

The addition of love, however, brings trans- formation. Andrew Lloyd-Webber was right when he said that it changes everything. Adding to everyday relationships love for God brings joy, since loves drives away the critical spirit and helps to see others as God sees them. Adding love for the Lord Jesus Christ brings holiness, since Christian men and women want to be like him. Adding love for the Bible brings truth, since Christians read the Word of God, drink in its teaching and delight in its message. Adding love for the world brings mission, since Christians have a message that brings salvation and indescribable joy. Finally, adding love for other Christians brings unity, since through the practical exercising of love, Christians discover that God has bound them together in a living, vital commu- nity.

The man-made barriers that divide the world cannot prevent the immediate sense of unity that Christ- ians experience when they first meet other Christians. Irrespective of skin-colour or denominational back- ground, Christians are drawn to one another by the same life-giving power that God the Father used to draw Christian people to his Son. When someone becomes a Christian, they experience *koinonia* straightaway. They share something in common with others. With God, they share his life and salvation. With God's people, they share his love.

Jennifer: Transient communities, case 2

There are many turning points in life that can challenge our very identity, and become a time of vulnerability and isolation.

Jennifer is in her early twenties, and newly graduated. She has found herself alone after university. She has never experienced this isolation before, having gone from home to university Halls of Residence, then to a house share with four other students. Whilst she has stayed where she is, in a small Midlands town, her friends have moved away to the brighter lights. She has discovered that although the place is the same, everything feels unfamiliar and awkward. She has in one go lost routine, friends, responsibilities and direction, and realises that she needs to rebuild. She has discovered, however, that our society offers very few anchors or supports for people to grasp easily in this situation. Perhaps, she thinks, her new job, which she starts next week, will give her a structure, but she has already passed through a series of unsatisfying temporary jobs. Her degree has proved not to be a passport to success, and she has begun to worry about paying off her £12,000 student loan. Returning home is not an option.

Has the loving community John outlined in his letter anything to offer a person like Jennifer? Will she see such talk of community as being merely a crutch, the mark of her failure to take hold of her life? If she went into the church at the bottom of her street, she would be struck by the fact that most of the congregation seems to her to be old – in its forties or fifties, or even older. What would attract her to its fellowship? Can love change everything for Jennifer?

5

Love in action

What do an ape and a human have in common? Biologists tell us that ninety-eight per cent of our genetic make up is similar to that of the depressed creature we may see in a zoo. Of course our differences outweigh the similarities, all the wonder and tragedy of being human, despite our instinctive ability to peel bananas. Who is the odd one out in the following list – a Chinese national, a Turk, a British citizen, or a Mormon? The answer is the last, who does not drink tea.

A moment's thought makes us realise that there are many ways of grouping people together – our common humanity, our choice of hot beverage, whether we are the kind of person who persists to reading the fifth chapter of a book. Some groupings we might suggest are superficial or plain stupid; some might touch the very core of our identity.

At the heart of *koinonia* is the basic word *koinos* or 'common.' 'Fellowshippers' or *koinonoi* are those who hold something in common – something very real and important.

We have already explored how the kind of 'in-common-ness' that is our focus is not a natural one. We are not talking about people who have the same age group, gender, interests, education, or race in common. Rather we are talking about those who share in the saving grace of the three members of the Holy Trinity. Made alive by the word and will of the Father, redeemed by the blood of the Son, and indwelt by the presence of the same Holy Spirit, we have come to share in a common salvation. We also share in a common inheritance as we look forward to participating (another *koinonia* word) in the glory, the sheer splendour, of God.

To share these things in common means that we share them with each other. So our vertical link with God links us horizontally with each other, a link that is unbreakable and undeniable. In the words of our foundation text in 1 John 1:3: 'Our fellowship is with the Father and with his Son, Jesus Christ.' Note the word *our*, and if that does not make the point strongly enough, John goes on to spell it out, 'we have fellowship with one another' (1:7). Fellowship with God is the source from which fellowship among Christians springs; and fellowship with God is the end towards which Christian fellowship is the means. James I. Packer comments: 'We should not, therefore, think of our fellowship with other Christians as a spiritual luxury, an optional addition to the exercises of private devotion. We should recognise rather that such fellowship is a spiritual necessity; for God has made us in such a way that our fellowship with Himself is fed by our fellowship with fellow Christians.'[106]

If fellowship with God puts us into fellowship with each other, where does fellowship with each other put us? It places us into a relationship of inescapable and reciprocal responsibility for each other, what the New Testament describes literally as 'one-another-ness.' It is a two-sided relationship of giving and taking, of mutual care and consideration.

This responsibility arises from the fundamental fact that we belong to one another. We are our brother's keeper precisely because we are brothers and sisters. To use another New Testament image, we are the Body of Christ, pointing to an organic and vital union with Christ and with each other. 'In Christ we who are many form one body, and each member belongs to all the rest'[107]

Love at the heart: Be devoted to one another

This 'one-another-ness' is mentioned fifty-eight times in the New Testament. We have already considered the fact that love for one another lies at the heart of *koinonia*; everything else is an out-working of that. The letter to the church in Rome therefore instructs us: 'Be devoted to one another in brotherly love'[108]

The picture here is of a family. This is an entirely appropriate metaphor to use of the Christian fellowship – it adds the dimensions of warmth, tenderness, concern, and loyalty. The term 'brotherly love' translates the Greek word *philadelphia*, a term that describes the affectionate bond which should exist between brothers and sisters. The word 'brothers' (Greek: *adelphoi*) is used around 230 times to describe the Christian family of brothers and sisters.

The command 'be devoted' translates another Greek word that conveys the thought of natural affection, not an affection that circumstances prompt. In other words, the affection is innately there because of a relationship in which we find ourselves. This is important to understanding the Apostle's command here. Our love for each other is not to be something either superficial or official. Our love is not to be simply the 'liking' of people who attend the same place of worship, or the kind of deference we give to fellow employees or to our boss. Rather the Apostle is saying that our love for our fellow believers should take on the same character as the love we have for members of our natural families. Dr. Martin Lloyd-Jones suggests that a good translation might be 'love your brothers in faith as if they were blood brothers.'

When I was a boy I loved the stories of Tom Sawyer and Huckleberry Finn. These two young adventurers signed a pact with their own blood, committing themselves to one another. Blood brothers would do anything for one another – even die for each other. Christians are blood brothers and sisters in the wonderful sense that 'in [Christ] we have redemption through his blood, the forgiveness of sins' – it is his blood, not ours, that binds us together.[109]

How are we to live as those who are devoted to one another in brotherly love? The Apostle is clearly speaking of something very practical, not a fuzzy feeling. We are to remind ourselves that we have been 'born again', that we have a new nature and that we share this with our fellow believers. Remind yourself of that as you think of them, warts and all. You have started a new life and you have come into a new family; and so have all the rest. We are all accepted in as 'members of the God's household.'[110] We have received 'the Spirit of adoption … by which we cry, "Abba, Father".'[111]

This means that we treat each other as our own. Have you noticed that you will put up with things from your own family that you would not tolerate elsewhere? We are always more tolerant of our own children's behaviour than we are of other people's. As Martyn Lloyd-Jones put it, 'We defend our own; we make excuses; we are always on the defensive of our own; we can always understand what they are doing. And Paul is saying that this should be equally true of our relationship to one another as Christians.'[112]

We of course need to distinguish between liking and loving here. Even in our natural families there are some we like better than others. In the Christian family we are not told to like everyone to the same degree, but we are told to love to the same degree. In fact, one test of the new life of God within us will be this, that we find ourselves with a better understanding of and a deeper affection for our fellow Christian than we have for relatives who are not Christians.

Loving one another in brotherly (and sisterly) love will involve 'honouring' each other. The two ideas of devotion and honour are linked in Romans 12:10, 'Be devoted to one another in brotherly love. Honour one another above yourselves.' I have wondered for a long time why the Apostle so closely links these two expressions of love. Could it be that we too easily take each other for granted? That familiarity breeds contempt? This would explain why we all need to be told to take a lead in offering respect to each other. I need to make sure that I am always first to accord honour and respect to my brother or sister in Christ. He is not saying that we should fight with each other as to who is going to open the door first for the other. You can just imagine that happening – sometimes we do that for a laugh. One says, 'O no, you first'; the other responds, 'No, I got here first – you go first.' You could stay there all day having that kind of conversation!

Honouring one another does not mean dishonouring or putting yourself down. Nor does it mean failing to take a lead on an issue or in a situation. Rather, honouring each other is born in a heart that sees itself as God sees it. This attitude is expressed in promoting, building up, and serving each other in the family of God.

Love at the heart: Accept one another

The Apostle brings out another aspect of the common link with each other in *koinonia* near the end of his letter to the church in Rome: 'Accept one another, then, just as Christ accepted you, in order to bring praise to God.'[113]

Have you ever found yourself on the wrong side of a door in the middle of the night? There is an extraordinary amount of rejection in the world today. Children can feel rejected by their parents; wives by their husbands; the poor, the homeless and the unemployed by society. Among God's people, however, there is to be no rejection of one another. Sometimes, even among Christians, acceptance is conditional upon things that you do or do not do. I was once pastor of a church where some of the people accepted newcomers only if the men attended in a three-piece suit and the women dressed appropriately (which meant wearing hats). I actually think those people acted like this by default; they had never really thought through their position in the light of Scripture. It is possible to make our acceptance of others a conditional thing, introducing into the equation rules and regulations about all kinds of unimportant things, which can easily be a barrier. It can create false guilt, promote a judgemental spirit and destroy personal freedom – freedom to be what I am in Christ.

The Apostle's picture of living in common with each other is very different from this attitude. We are to 'welcome', 'receive' or 'accept' one another. To work this out in practice is both a negative and a positive activity.

Let us first look at the negative side of accepting one another: we will not 'judge' each other. To judge another is a violation of the principle of accepting them. 'Let us stop passing judgement on one another', warns the Apostle.[114]

We pass judgement when we jump to the wrong conclusions, when we are critical and condemning, and when we misinterpret or misrepresent. In churches both in Rome and in Corinth one of the big disputes between believers was whether it was right to eat food bought in the market, which had previously been offered to an idol. People were taking sides on this issue and making it a matter of principle, and a matter of fellowship, which it was not. Paul's answer was to point out that the Bible gave no clear guidance about this issue – no sin was involved. Instead, everyone was to be 'convinced in their own minds' about the matter.[115]

We will not 'keep on biting and devouring each other' or 'provoking and envying each other.'[116] We will not 'lie to each other.'[117] Nor will we 'slander' or speak against or 'grumble against' each other.[118]

Now for the positive side of accepting each other. It will mean 'bearing with one another in love'; being 'kind and compassionate to one another, forgiving each other, just as in Christ God forgave you.'[119]

These words tell us how to receive new Christians. Often people will join us who come with a murky past. How are we to react? The answer is clear – receive them as Christ has received us.[120] They also tell us how we are to receive weak Christians, that is, Christians whose background means they have oversensitive consciences. We are to receive them without destroying them.[121] 'We also who are strong,' writes the Apostle, 'ought to bear with the failings of the weak and not please ourselves.'[122]

How are we to receive sinning Christians? We are to forgive 'each other, just as God in Christ forgave' us.[123] How are we to receive difficult Christians? 'Be patient, bearing with one another in love.'[124]

Only as we meet with each other can we express this kind of membership to each other, with its mutual caring. Therefore, we are to receive one another as we meet in public worship.

We find the call to 'greet one another', issued as a reciprocal duty, emphasised in the New Testament (it is repeated five times, to be exact). Furthermore, our greeting of each other is not to be formal or perfunctory – the mere performance of a duty. The Apostle urges, in Romans 16:16: 'Greet one another with a holy kiss.' We may choose to replace that with the hearty handshake or the warm embrace but the force of it remains. The point is that we should learn to demonstrate appropriate physical affection towards one another. It should become part of our body language. Such affection can create oneness, unity, and even spiritual and psychological healing.

We are to receive one another as we meet around the Lord's Table (see chapter nine). Paul's criticism of the Corinthian church was their selfishness as they gathered, the fact that they looked out for themselves and did not acknowledge the Lord's body, that is, his people. One person would get drunk while another went hungry. We are also to receive one another into our own homes. 'Offer hospitality to one another without grumbling', Peter enjoins.[125]

Paul asserts the principle that we are to 'serve one another in love.'[126] Service is indeed the highest expression of love. Such a service can be physical or spiritual.

Physical service

Remember the example of our Lord Jesus, recorded in John 13, where he washed the disciples' feet. Jesus knew it was the night of his betrayal and that the very next morning he would suffer on the cross for the sins of the world. We might have expected him to have been preoccupied with his imminent sufferings. Yet we find him taking the time to perform a duty – the washing of the feet of guests – which was usually left to the lowest servant in the household. He was aware of his dignity ('He had come from God and was returning to God'[127]), but he had come to serve. They had been arguing among themselves as to which of them was the greatest. None of them had volunteered to do the servant's job. Then Jesus, the greatest of them all by infinity, became their servant.

Love is not merely sentiment and emotion. It takes more than sentiment to wash the dirty feet of rough fishermen, ignoring the smell and indignity of it all. Love is real service rather than sentiment. Serving means doing helpful deeds for one another. Like the Apostle Paul, who lit a fire for his shipwrecked fellow passengers. Like the American senator, who heard on the car radio of a political opponent's admission to hospital. He rushed there to see what he could do. He found the switchboard jammed with calls from well-wishers and no one available to operate it. Quietly, he got behind the phones and stayed all night to answer them, only to slip away in the morning.

We must not spiritualise the forms of physical service, downplaying the practical and nitty-gritty. That service is there to be done by those who simply want to be like Jesus.

Spiritual service

Spiritual service is that in which we use our spiritual gifts to 'serve others':[128] where we 'instruct one another',[129] using whatever level of insight we have; where we 'carry one each other's burdens';[130] where we comfort and 'encourage one another.'[131]

Serving one another usually requires no special talent or ability. It does, however, take a servant attitude to want to serve others, as well as an observant eye and mind to see what needs to be done.

Fellowship with one another involves loving one another, and loving one another is a very practical thing. It means being devoted to one another as a family; it involves accepting each other and serving one another.

You can see why it is that in a fragmented society, where everyone is out for number one, the gospel community should offer an attractive and beautiful alternative to the world.

Lesley: A reminder of traditional ties

Lesley is a part-time cleaner in her late forties, married with grown-up son. She has lived in the same area of suburban south-west London since childhood. Lesley has lifelong women friends whom she sees regularly. They arrange frequent days out to the coast for themselves and their husbands. Her son lives locally and they go and see a film together every Saturday morning when seats are half price.

Compared with others, her focus is narrow and her circle is tightly knit. She does not have great opportunities or ambitions, but gains much support and satisfaction from the regularity of her life and the people with whom she shares it.

Lesley has faced real trauma, losing her second son in a car accident when he was in Year Four at school. The experience prompted her to reconsider her beliefs and priorities. She has managed to retain an openness towards and acceptance of life's unpredictability.

What might Lesley have to offer in the practical out-working of love – in devotion to one another, acceptance of each other, and serving one another? How might she benefit from receiving these same demonstrations of love?

6

'He ain't heavy, he's my brother'

At the heart of the experience of loneliness is its perception of isolation and separation. This may include the sense of being left out, of being rejected, of being estranged, of not being understood, of being abandoned. Loneliness involves the feeling that there is no one responsive to our deep human hunger for support and caring.

The increasing incidence of suicide among young men is blamed on loneliness and their inability to socialise. We saw that the rock band R.E.M. addressed the subject of suicide in their song *Everybody Hurts*. It focuses on the loneliness that often drives people to the verge of despair and self-murder. Their song urged the lonely to hold on and not lose hope, even when their days and nights are long.

We have been arguing from the New Testament that its vision of *koinonia* or fellowship is the antidote to the loneliness that blights so many lives in the modern world. The ultimate answer to the search for identity and community, which we see everywhere in our society, is to be found in that new community which is being built by Jesus Christ. Here, people from very diverse backgrounds, of every race, of both sexes, find a common life and a common bond. What brings them together and unites them is not natural but supernatural; it is not superficial but real; it is not theoretical but practical.

Consider the words of Jesus's closest follower, John: 'Dear children, let us not love with words or tongue but with actions and in truth.'[132] What does this new Christian relationship look like? We have explored how at its most basic it is a love relationship. We have also seen that it is a family relationship, for Christians share the same nature since they have been 'born again' into the same family. This throws us into a relationship of mutual love. We cannot sit back and expect others to make all the moves – there is no issue about who must make the first move. In this new family we are all to accept responsibility to act proactively in order to demonstrate Christian love. There is nothing more practical than Paul's command: 'Carry each other's burdens.'[133]

Supporting each other

Many people in our society carry a crushingly heavy and very real burden. This might be a burden of debt, which may be due to unexpected circumstances or bad judgement. It may be a burden of guilt because of habits, relationships in the past or present, or perceived failures. The burden could be illegitimate guilt, as when, for example, a child grows up blaming themselves for the violence they have seen at home, or for physical or   sexual abuse they have suffered. The burden might be pain. Perhaps someone has just had a terrifying diagnosis from a doctor. Maybe a wife feels trapped in a loveless marriage. Possibly the sheer pressure of work and the long hours involved have pushed an employee to breaking point. Such workers, managers or executives are often reluctant to admit their struggles because to do so would be to admit failure or invite demotion or dismissal. When we meet with our colleagues from work, when we sit with our fellow-worshippers in church, when we join our friends at an event, we have absolutely no idea what burdens they may be carrying.

How are we to treat others then? Paul is clear – we are to 'carry each other's burdens.' This command is especially for Christians and the way we treat each other, but it has relevance to our Christian witness to others. This is so since the command to 'love one another' is coupled with two other New Testament commands, to 'love your neighbour' (anyone in need) and to 'love your enemy' (which speaks for itself). If we think at first that this burden bearing is going to be an easy ride, these related commands show us that we are way off track.

We cannot get away from the task by assuming that it is for the specialist and the professional. One of the New Testament terms for a Christian leader, it is true, is the word 'pastor', which means 'shepherd.' The 'Chief Shepherd' of God's flock, his people, is Jesus himself. He delegates to under-shepherds the task of tending 'the flock of God.' The New Testament model is that the 'pastor' is a teacher who 'feeds the flock' by teaching them, and who enables the flock to take care of themselves. So, for example, in his letter to the Ephesians (in chapter 4) the Apostle talks of 'pastor-teachers' whom Christ gives as a gift to the churches 'to prepare God's people for works of service, so that the body of Christ may be built up.'[134] The purpose of spiritual gifts, bestowed on each one of God's people, is, however, that the members of Christ's body 'should have equal concern for each other.'[135] Pastoral ministry is to be a shared ministry of the entire congregation. So Paul tells the Galatian church members to 'carry each other's burdens'; he tells the Thessalonians to 'help the weak'; and he tells the church in Rome, 'We who are strong ought to bear with the failings of the weak.'[136]

None of us likes to admit that we are ever weak. We all know people who seem always on the edge of breakdown; we consider them to be rather weak and ineffective, and we don't want people to think that we could be like that. Yet the fact of the matter is that every one of us is weak at some time. R.E.M.'s song is quite right at this point ... everybody weeps at some point. We need to remember that, and we need to learn to have much more honesty and understanding. Men particularly find it well nigh impossible to express their feelings and work through their emotions and as for admitting need, forget it!

Here the Bible is refreshingly direct. It has no superheroes – there is no attempt to disguise human frailty or failure. When Paul first went to preach to proud and sophisticated Corinth he tells us that it was 'in weakness and fear and with much trembling.'[137] At a later point in his life, he and his friends admit to being 'under great pressure, far beyond our ability to endure, so that we despaired even of life.'[138] He is 'hard pressed… perplexed …persecuted …struck down.'[139] He speaks of his 'thorn in the flesh' and his utter 'weakness.'[140] No wonder he spoke of the need for being shored up by the encouragement of his fellow Christians.[141]

In his excellent book, *No Longer Alone*, Bruce Milne[142] points to our Lord's experience of weakness.

> We see Him being assaulted by the arresting officers; whipped by the guard; crucified in utter weakness; lifted up before the eyes of a jeering, mocking mob; deserted by friends and all in order to accomplish our salvation.

On the cross He cries 'I thirst.' The One through whom the very oceans were formed cries out in the agony of dehydration for the relief of a few drops of water. Here is the Creator in His weakness dependent upon the whim of His own creatures. At the height of His agony His identification with us goes so far that He becomes the bearer of our sin and the object of God's wrath. At that moment He cries out, 'My God, My God why have you forsaken me?' There He experienced 'a helplessness, which has had no equal in the long history of humanity.'

We also see this principle at work in His earthly ministry in the calling of his disciples. He chose the number twelve as surely a deliberate echo of the number of the tribes of Israel, and as an expression of Jesus' consciousness that through His mission He was to inaugurate the new covenant between God and man and 'reconstitute the covenant community as the people of the Messiah, the new Israel.' He chose them with a view to training them for their future responsibilities. As leaders of the new community of the kingdom of God they were called to be 'with Him' and hence to be equipped to be 'sent out' by Him.

Bruce Milne then argues that the disciples had a secondary ministry which was directed to Jesus himself. Although the basis in the text is not a strong one, the fact that 'He had to be made like his brothers and sisters in every way,'[143] and was able 'to sympathise with our weaknesses',[144] suggests that it is valid to think of Jesus sometimes finding strength in others. In the garden of Gethsemane Jesus's plea to his disciples, 'My soul is very sorrowful, even to death … watch with me,' suggests a strong longing for human comradeship, a need for fellowship as he experiences the agony of his temptation. Jesus may have been thinking in these terms, suggests

Milne, when he characterises the twelve as those who have 'continued with me in my trials.'

John Wesley said that there is no such thing as a solitary Christian. If we are determined to go it alone we are attempting more than the Apostle Paul or even our Lord himself did. We cannot dodge responsibility for our own spiritual growth, nor can we blame others for our own sin. We do, however, need the help and companionship of others in our Christian walk. Any talk of holiness or spirituality that does not also talk of learning to relate to my Christian brothers and sisters and carry their burdens is unrealistic and unbiblical. No wonder we are encouraged to 'bear each other's burdens.'

Praying for each other

The blunt and practical James, in his letter, tells us to 'Pray for each other.'[145]

Often when we are in trouble, we find comfort in the promise that someone will pray for us. Such a promise of course has to be matched by practical action. It is also true that when people pray with us through a trial we are facing or a decision we have to make, this can deepen their commitment to us and their relationship with us.

Jesus' practice shows us that if we really care for people we will pray for them. While on earth, we are told, he prayed on one occasion for Peter, and now, in heaven, he prays for his people. In Acts chapter 4 we have a beautiful picture of the early church gathered for an impromptu prayer time to celebrate the Apostles' return from prison and trial. The Apostle Paul is another example of this attitude. He both prayed for others and regularly asked others to pray for him.

In praying for others, what are we to pray about? Our immediate tendency is to pray about immediate issues or problems which people are facing. There is, of course, nothing wrong with this – in fact the Bible urges us to 'cast all our burdens' on the Lord in this way. We are, however, limiting prayer if we only pray for these things. Bruce Milne writes: 'One is tempted to think that the only sure way to get Christians to pray for one is to fall under a bus and be carted off to hospital.'[146]

Fortunately the Apostle Paul sets us an example of how to pray others. He concentrates his prayers on their spiritual growth rather than on their immediate bodily needs (not that these are unimportant). Is there something we should learn from this priority for our prayers today, so that our prayers for others are sustained and consistent? Do you have people whom you pray for regularly? Are there those who pray for you? Do you have a prayer partner? One of the most exciting innovations that has emerged within the contemporary church has been the setting up of 'prayer triplets', where a small group of people commit themselves to pray together for each other and for others beyond the group.

Confessing our sins to each other

The ever direct James tells us not only to pray for one another, but to 'confess [our] sins to each other.'[147]

Primarily we confess our sins to the Lord. Forgiveness is ours through the work that Christ completed once and for all on Calvary. We need, however, to come repeatedly to confess specific sins and seek renewal of our relationship with him. On the other hand, where the sins in question have been committed against fellow Christians, and are of such a nature that they are aware

of these sins, and this awareness has broken our fellowship with them, then we must confess those sins.

We need to be cautious here. All sins, whether of
thought, word, or deed, must be confessed to God,
because of course he sees them all.[148] We need to remember however that human beings do not share the
omniscience of God. People hear our words and see our
actions but they cannot read our hidden thoughts. It is,
therefore, social sins of word and act that we must confess to our fellows, not sinful thoughts we have had
about them. In their desire to be open and honest some
believers, with more zeal than sense, go too far in this
matter. To say 'I'm sorry I was rude to you' or 'I'm sorry
I showed off in front of you' is right; but not 'I'm afraid
I've had jealous or lustful thoughts about you all day.'
Such a confession does not help; it only embarrasses. In
fact this puts up a barrier where there may not have been
one before. If the sin remains secret in the mind and does
not erupt into words or deeds, confess it to God alone.
The rule is always that secret sins must be confessed
secretly (to God), private sins must be confessed priv-
ately (to the injured party), and public sins must be
confessed openly to the congregation. Our text from
James is to be seen as a command to those who have
mutually offended one another to confess those sins to
one another.

There is almost nothing more difficult to do than this.
'I'm sorry' must be about the most difficult words to say
in any language. How many churches divide and how
many relationships break because these words refuse to
be spoken! Our pride is often hurt by our failure and
does not want to own up. When we apologise we are
reduced to our real size, to what we really are – poor and
needy sinners living by grace alone. When we say 'I'm
sorry' we are being real before our Christian brother or

sister, and in that moment of confession, as we present ourselves to them in our weakness and vulnerability, we invite them to become real too. We give them the opportunity to step out from behind their curtains of sham and pretence and to stand with us in the presence of the Lord, waiting for his grace.

This is a rare Christian grace. D.L. Moody, the famous American evangelist of the nineteenth century, demonstrated it in action. When establishing his home in Northfield, Massachusetts, Moody was anxious to have a lawn like those he had greatly admired in England. One day however his two sons, Paul and Will, let the horses loose from the barn. They galloped over his precious lawn and ruined it. Moody lost his temper with them. But the boys never forgot how, after they had gone to bed that night, they heard his heavy footsteps as he approached and entered their room. Laying a hand on their heads, he said to them: 'I want you to forgive me; that wasn't the way Christ taught.' On another occasion, a theological student interrupted him during an address and Moody snapped an irritated retort. Let J.C. Pollock describe what happened at the end of the sermon

> He reached his close. He paused. Then he said: 'Friends, I want to confess before you all that I made a great mistake at the beginning of this meeting. I answered my young brother down there foolishly. I ask God to forgive me. I ask him to forgive me.' And before anyone realised what was happening the world's most famous evangelist had stepped off the platform, dashed across to the anonymous youth and taken him by the hand. As another present said, 'The man of iron will proved that he had mastered the hardest of all earth's languages, "I am sorry."' Someone else called it 'the greatest single thing I ever saw D.L. Moody do.'

This kind of response evokes a dimension of relationship with each other and honour for one another that is beyond anything that comes naturally to any of us. Persuasion will not get people treating each other like this; legislation cannot do it; coercion will fail to achieve it. It takes the Spirit of God to make people with the new nature to do this. Where such a spirit pervades even a small Christian community it will have an impact on its society as a whole. This happened in England after the great Evangelical Awakening in the eighteenth century, resulting in widespread social reform and ultimately a worldwide abolition of slavery. It can happen again.

Roger: Beyond community

Roger provides an example of how it is possible to exist very easily and ordinarily beyond the bounds of any community, untroubled by the cares of others.

He is single and in his early forties. After rising quickly in business, he is now financial director for a textile importer. Roger owns a large house in opulent Surrey that he shares with paying lodgers. He avoids deeper commitment with women because he finds them 'high maintenance' relationships.

He works and plays hard, particularly enjoying the adrenaline rush of surfing. His participation in others' lives is limited to visiting his mother and sister in Cornwall and in sharing banter with his lodgers, with whom he is popular. He knows no one in his neighbourhood (he even shops for his food via the Internet) and has very little concept of community – and no need for it.

Roger does no one any harm and is happy enough. Taking on the cares of others would undoubtedly upset the equilibrium of his life and trouble him. In what ways would the command to bear each other's burdens apply to him? Does the church have any responsibility to Roger, when so many people are in obvious need?

7

Meeting together

The signature tune of life today is our search for community.

The popular 1980s' TV show *Cheers* continues to re-run. Its popularity lies in the fact that it touches a chord deep down in the human psyche. The bar it portrays is a place where life brings regular random encounters with friends, not just occasional, carefully scheduled lunches with them. Here there are spats and rivalries, yes, but in this bar, grievances are usually heard in short order and tensions thus resolved.

In his book *Megatrends 2000*, John Naisbitt points out that, with each new wave of technological advancements, people seek a compensatory human touch. Despite an explosion in sales of high-tech VCRs, for instance, human beings still need the 'high touch' experience of going to a movie theatre with their friends. Even though airline computers daily juggle hundreds of air-traffic schedules, along with thousands of seating options, every major carrier has set up a telephone reservation system that affords the personal touch of speaking to a human being about a particular flight and a specific seat.[149]

In Western society, we brush shoulders with more and more people, but nearly all our relationships are with strangers. More people, it is said, are alive in our present generation than the total of all who have lived in human history and are now dead. Yet in our crowded planet we struggle to have relationships of any depth and quality. We have unprecedented choice and mobility (at least those of us in the rich West) yet all we touch seems to turn to dust, if we measure life by relationships rather than mere possessions. As Michael Schluter and David Lee write: 'We meet many more people, but less frequently. We still have friends and families, but on the whole these relationships are fewer, more intermittent, less stable.'[150]

All around us there are people in need of encouragement, love and friendship. In the letter to the Hebrews we are urged; 'let us encourage one another',[151] and to 'encourage one another daily.'[152] The Greek word *parakaleo* variously translates into English as encourage, comfort, exhort, beseech, and console. Jesus uses this precise word of the Holy Spirit. He is the *parakletos*, that is, the One who comes alongside to help, support, comfort and strengthen us in our relationship with God. Encouragement can also be defined as 'helping someone become greater for God.'

There are many examples of encouragement in the Bible. At a low point in King David's life we read about his friend Jonathan who 'went to David at Horesh and helped him to find strength in God.'[153] When the Apostle Paul was first converted, the help of Barnabas put him on his feet and enabled him to get into his world-changing ministry.[154] Barnabas was dubbed 'The son of encouragement.'[155] Paul writes of his own example: 'For you know that we dealt with you as a father deals with his own children, encouraging, comforting and urging you to live lives worthy of God,' and he goes on to urge them, 'therefore encourage one another and build each other up.'[156]

Where are people to find encouragement? All we have discovered so far about encouraging one another is quite academic unless we are meeting each other on a regular basis. The Bible links meeting together with encouraging one another.

We are to meet together to worship

'Let us not give up meeting together as some are in the habit of doing,' the Apostle writes in Hebrews.[157] God may save us one by one but he then puts us into groups. One by one, we enter the kingdom but then we find that the kingdom is a community, a family, a body. The Hebrews passage teaches us that we cannot grow spiritually, in the way God means us to, in isolation from one another. In fact, it suggests that we will be discouraged and easily knocked off course if we do not have companionship along the way. In the letter to the Hebrews we find Christians described as siblings in the same family, partners in the same enterprise, and members of the same household.

The problem the writer addresses in the letter is of some believers who are acting as if they are pious particles with no need of others; they are deserting or forsaking the worship gatherings of God's people.

From the earliest days the Christian movement recognised the need for corporate gatherings for worship. We can see this when we read Acts chapter 2, which is about the birthday of the Christian Church. Peter proclaims the message and a large number of people receive it. What happens next? These same people 'devoted themselves to the Apostles' teaching, to the fellowship, to the breaking of bread and to the prayers.'[158] They addressed the issues raised by needs within their group, and they praised God together. They saw the necessity for teaching from accredited people, and for gathering corporately for praise and prayer. Everybody was searching for genuine community and for authentic relationships of love. In his book, *The Contemporary Christian*, John Stott lists three secular challenges to the church of Jesus Christ today. These are the quest for transcendence, for significance and for community. If the world's search for transcendence is a challenge to the church's worship, and the search for significance is a challenge to its teaching, then the search for community is a challenge to the church's fellowship. John Stott points out:

> We proclaim that God is love, and that Jesus Christ offers true community. We insist that the church is part of the gospel. God's purpose, we say, is not merely to save isolated individuals, and so perpetuate their loneliness, but to create a new society, even a new humanity, in which racial, national, social and sexual barriers have been abolished. Moreover, this new community of Jesus dares to present itself as the true alternative society, which eclipses the values and standards of the world.[159]

Bishop Stephen Neill expressed well the impact of Jesus' love experienced through Christian community:

> Within the fellowship of those who are bound together by personal loyalty to Jesus Christ, the relationship of love reaches an intimacy and intensity unknown elsewhere. Friendship between the friends of Jesus of Nazareth is unlike any other friendship. This ought to be normal experience within the Christian community…That in existing Christian congregations it is so rare is a measure of the failure of the church as a whole to live up to the purpose of its Founder for it. Where it is experienced, especially across

the barriers of race, nationality and language, it is one of the most convincing evidences of the continuing activity of Jesus among men.[160]

We are to meet together in homes

To love means to share, and sharing includes a welcome in our homes. In Acts chapter 2 the early church not only met in the Temple courts; they also met 'from house to house.' Luke, the writer of Acts, records: 'Every day they continued to meet together in the Temple courts. They broke bread in their homes and ate together with glad and sincere hearts ...'[161]

Jesus himself was dependent on the hospitality of friends, especially that of Mary, Martha and Lazarus of Bethany. When he sent out the Twelve and the Seventy he expected them to be given hospitality[162] and he regarded the refusal of hospitality as the equivalent of a rejection of their message. In Matthew chapter 25 he tells a parable in which there is a clear reference to hospitality, 'I was a stranger and you invited me in.' Here giving or withholding of hospitality, when we are in a position to offer it, is a decisive indication of the presence or absence of real spiritual life.

We should not be surprised to find that the New Testament urges us to open our homes to others. 'Practise hospitality!' we are urged.[163] 'Offer hospitality to one another without grumbling,' we are commanded.[164] This latter reference is set in a context where Peter is speaking about spiritual gifts. It means that we cannot complain that we have not received a gift of the Holy Spirit if he has given us a home, into which we can welcome other people. A home is a gift of God, which he wants us to invest in the interests of the kingdom of God. If we fail to use our homes in this way then we really have no grounds for complaining about a lack of fellowship or friendship in our local church. Beyond the fringes of our churches there are countless people who are in need of genuine friendship, a friendship sealed by our willingness to open our homes and our hearts to them.

Right here is the greatest gospel opportunity that presents itself to us in the early twenty-first century. The challenge is to offer unconditional friendship to people who are lonely. It is a challenge to offer them a place of refuge from the storms of life, a secure place in a dog-eat-dog world.

Years ago, at the start of my ministry, I read words that confronted me, and I have never forgotten them: 'The neighbourhood bar is possibly the best counterfeit there is to the fellowship Christ wants to give His church. It's an imitation, dispensing liquor instead of grace, escape rather than reality, but it is a permissive, accepting, and inclusive fellowship. It is unshockable. It is democratic. You can tell people secrets and they usually don't tell others or even want to. The bar flourishes not because most people are alcoholics, but because God has put into the human heart the desire to know and be known, to love and be loved, and so many seek a counterfeit at the price of a few beers.'[165]

The writer went on to say that he wholeheartedly believed that Jesus wants church fellowships in which people can walk in and admit openly that they have had it, that they are sunk, that they are beaten. Who are people to turn to if their spouse is an alcoholic, if their son has just confessed that he is in a gay relationship, or they discover their daughter is addicted to heroin? It is too easy to list the crises that face very many people – redundancy, coping with life after jail, a pregnant underage daughter, the discovery that a trusted friend has abused one's child.

'Do you know what they need?' Bruce Larson continued. 'They need a shelter. A place of refuge. A few folks who can help them, listen to them, introduce them once again to "the Father of mercies and the God of all comfort; who comforts us in all our affliction."'[166] I wonder whether our churches are making any effort to be this kind of fellowship. Chuck Swindoll writes: 'Christianity may be "like a mighty army," but we handle our troops in a weird way. We're the only outfit I've ever heard of who shoots their wounded.' He concluded: 'What we need are shelters for storm victims; hospitals for those who hurt; healing centres that specialise in wounded hearts, broken dreams, and shipwrecked souls.'

We do well to remember John's words in his first letter

> And so we know and rely on the love God has for us. God is love. Those who live in love live in God, and God in them. In this way, love is made complete among us so that we will have confidence on the day of judgement, because in this world we are like him. There is no fear in love. But perfect love drives out fear, because fear has to do with punishment. The one who fears is not made perfect in love.[167]

If we take these words seriously about the church as a shelter, living out God's love, then it is quite clear what is involved:

- A willingness to go the distance for someone in trouble. Jesus called that willingness, 'going the second mile'. His actual words were, 'If someone asks you to go one mile with them, go with them two.'
- An attitude of loving compassion for those in need.

- An availability to help in practical, tangible ways.
- An ability to help people feel needed and important in this high-tech, contemporary society of ours that makes us acutely aware of our insignificance.

Is your home a haven for the storm-tossed or a monument to your selfishness?

We are to meet together in twos and threes

Jesus himself tells us, 'Where two or three come together in my name, there I am with them.'[168] An old Puritan adage puts it like this: 'Have communion with few, be intimate with one.' For *koinonia* (fellowship) to have depth, it must be limited in breadth. In the Bible's Wisdom books we are informed that, 'As iron sharpens iron, so one person sharpens another,'[169] and that 'Two are better than one, because they have a good return for their work. If they fall down, one can help the other up. But pity those who fall and have no friend to help them up!'[170] The theologian James I. Packer tells us that the Puritans used to ask God for a 'bosom friend' with whom they could share a full-scale prayer-partner relationship.

How do you make a friend out of a stranger? You say, 'Let's get together'; and then, sitting over a steaming cup of coffee, you begin to explore one another's personalities – you talk of your family and your friends, your interests, your hopes and your dreams. Gradually you paint a self-portrait in words, saying 'This is me, I want you to know me.' John Wesley once met a very serious person, who gave him this advice, 'Sir, you wish to serve God and go to heaven? Remember you cannot serve Him alone. You must therefore find companions or make them. The Bible knows nothing of solitary religion.' Wesley never forgot that wise counsel. Much later, he said, 'Christianity is a social religion. To turn it into a solitary religion is indeed to destroy it.'

We have a major problem in our modern relationships, expressed in our attitude to them. We think that because we share the same bed with someone we have a relationship with them. We think because we provide for our families that we have a relationship with them. We think that because we do things for our kids we have a relationship with them. We think that because we go to the same church or small group with people we have a relationship with them.

What has happened? We have lost the art of friendship. Yet friendship is basic to a whole series of human relationships. Is your wife or husband your friend? They should be. Are your children your friends? They should be. Do you have friends in church? You should have. Friendship was high on Jesus' list of priorities, as we find in one of the last bits of teaching he left us before his arrest, 'You are my friends if you do what I command.'[171]

The book of Proverbs talks of two kinds of friend. 'One who has many companions may come to ruin, but there is a friend who sticks closer than a brother or sister.'[172] The word 'sticks' is the same word used of a man cleaving to his wife,[173] of Ruth clinging to her mother-in-law[174] and of Israel cleaving to the Lord.[175] It has the sense of clinging to someone in affection and loyalty, two ideas that are the key to true friendship. The use of the word 'brother' (or 'sister') in comparing the value of friendship is significant. Many converts to Christianity have suffered painful alienation from their family members because of their faith.

There are two levels of friendship: our acquaintances, and our real friends. Derek Kidner, in his commentary says, 'Proverbs … is emphatic that a few close friends are better than a host of acquaintances, and stand in a class by themselves.'[176] Jesus showed this in his life. He ministered to the crowds, but he had a group of special friends, the twelve disciples, and from among these the inner circle of three, and from among them 'the disciple whom Jesus loved.'

One of the keys to a deep friendship is spending time in long conversations. Jesus had this type of relationship with his friends, the disciples. He said, 'I have called you friends, for everything that I learned from my Father I have made known to you.'[177]

Many of us do not seem to have time for such long conversations. We have so many things to do! When we have free time, we spend it on entertainment. Even when we are with friends, we want to be active, to go somewhere, play a game, watch a film, or whatever.

Conversations about truth can enrich our lives. Those who set apart time for enriching discussions on the important issues of life, bringing in rather than leaving out God, will rediscover the joy of truth. Through that, they will find a new depth of true personal fulfilment. Which is why Proverbs tells us, 'Whoever listens to a life-giving rebuke will be at home among the wise.'[178] The expression 'at home among the wise' implies that there is such a thing as a fellowship of wise people – people committed to the pursuit of knowledge. Sharing truth with one another can be such a great encouragement. The presence of common convictions amidst the confusion of today's world is an important ingredient of Christian friendship. As C.S. Lewis puts it in his book *The Four Loves*, 'Friendship … is born at the moment when one says to another "What! You too? I thought that no one but myself…"' The presence of people who seem to understand gives us courage to persevere.

We are to meet together for meals

When the first Christians met in homes they would 'eat together with glad and sincere hearts.'[179] Let us face it – the kind of relationships we have been talking about cannot be formed by regular church-going or even the larger midweek meetings of the church. Years ago, John Stott recognised this: 'There is always something unnatural and subhuman about large crowds. They tend to be aggregations rather than congregations – aggregations of unrelated persons. The larger they become, the less the individuals who compose them know and care about each other. Indeed crowds can perpetuate aloneness, instead of curing it.'[180] There is therefore a need for our congregations to be broken down into smaller units, such as the house meetings must have been in the early church. We cannot know more than around a dozen to twenty people in any church in any depth – we shall never get to know everyone, and that is perfectly all right. The early Christians met in the Temple and from 'house to house.' They shared their homes and they had meals together. To 'break bread' primarily meant to have a meal together. Christians sometimes simply remembered the Lord in the course of ordinary meals. By taking the fellowship meal out of homes into the church building, have we not made it unfriendly and formal? That is a question worth thinking about!

Jane: Time for me vs. time for others

Time. We are convinced we have less and less of it, and therefore we are all the more protective of it. We ring fence time for specific activities. We are less casual with time, reluctant to get to know people around us if it means possibly 'wasting time.' In fact, considering the labour-saving devices that fill our homes, we have – someone has worked out – half an hour longer per week than we used to. We also watch on average more than three hours of TV per day. Do we really have less time? Yet, we persist in believing and therefore feeling that our time is pressured.

Jane made an astonishing discovery about her time. She is forty-something, recently married to a Turkish man. After years of full-time work in occupational therapy, she recently negotiated a part-time contract. She now works three days per week. To her surprise, the benefit is more psychological than anything else. Now that she has the opportunity to have a lie-in four days a week, she finds she no longer needs one – on the weekend, let alone during the week.

The change to Jane's attitude is widespread. She is more relaxed about her time and therefore more generous with it. She willing to visit her mother more frequently and take her time in local shops chatting and getting to know people.

How could you change your attitude to your time, given that it is so much a matter of how we perceive it? Jane's change in hers came about through a shift in her circumstances, which led her to rethink the pattern of her life. Do you need to rethink your own patterns, even if you do not anticipate a life-change? How much does thinking about the church as fellowship and meeting together help you to order your individual circumstances, particularly over time?

8

Restoring one another

The artist applied his skill to a painstaking and tedious task – he was seeking to restore a faded work of art to its former glory. I was one of the onlookers standing and admiring his labour. I happened to be visiting a museum that allowed members of the general public to do this.

Over the years I have met people for whom restoring things is a hobby – whether it be an old car, a piece of old furniture, or an old home. I have vivid memories of having a meal with some folks on the outskirts of Philadelphia who had restored an old home where George Washington himself had once spent the night! They had painstakingly restored it to its Colonial original. All of us know what joy a bit of restoration can bring, whether it is sorting out a cluttered cupboard or meeting up with a long lost friend.

In the Bible we discover that the effects of sin on our world and in ourselves have been to leave us badly in need of restoring. This is why God has gone into the restoration business. We may get tired of watching his work, or may not even give it a glance in the first place. But he persists, nevertheless, in his committed task. To a society that had turned aside from him and experienced many years of spiritual barrenness and uselessness, God once said: 'I will restore to you the years which the swarming locust has eaten.'[181] He would make up for the years they had wasted.

To restore means to 'make whole' again. Jesus likened sin to a failure in our health (or wholeness). 'It is not the healthy who need a doctor, but the sick,' he said. 'I have not come to call the righteous, but sinners.'[182] To restore can also mean to 'turn back' which is also an aspect of repentance. In the letter of Titus[183] we read of 'renewal by the Holy Spirit.' Therefore, *to make new again* is another aspect of restoration. Taken together we can say that restoration means to *make whole*; to *turn back*; and to *make new*. It is a positive and a divine work since the Father, the Son and the Spirit are involved in the restoration business.

Restoration, however, is also the church's work. It is another vital part of *koinonia*, Christian fellowship.

All around us are the casualties of sin. We can all think of Christian people who once walked consistently with the Lord but who are today living far from him. We can think of Christian people whose sin became public, and who have gone elsewhere because they feel they are no longer welcome in the Christian community. Then there are those simply knocked out of the race by the circumstances of life. Such people need our ministry of restoration.

In Galatians we have an example of restoration in action: 'Let us not become conceited, provoking and envying each other. Brothers and sisters, if someone is caught in a sin, you who are spiritual should restore that person gently. But watch yourself, or you also may be tempted. Carry each other's burdens, and in this way you will fulfil the law of Christ.'[184] Before we can help others effectively, we must have a proper view of ourselves. To be conceited is to have a false view of ourselves. It poisons every other relationship we have, leading to 'provoking' others. This word has the idea of challenging someone. It implies that we are so sure of our superiority or our rightness that we want to demonstrate it. Conceit can also lead to 'envying' others, being jealous of their gifts or attainments. If we are conceited we shall never be able to help the spiritually weak or the morally wayward. Only those who have had their eyes opened to see their own sinfulness and unworthiness, as well as the value and importance of other people in the sight of God, are qualified to have a ministry of restoration.

Behind the ministry of restoration lies a principle we have already visited. 'Carry each others' burdens, and in this way you will fulfil the law of Christ.' The assumption behind this is that we all have burdens and God does not mean us to carry them alone. Some people, sadly, try to. There is a false view of holiness, which pro-jects the ideal Christian as one who is an omni-competent individualist, free from warts and blemishes and any traits that imply dependence on others. In this unreal view, we are all to strive to attain a level of all round spiritual competence that enables us to cope with any circumstance, overcome any obstacle, resist any temptation and experience a life of unbroken victory over sin and Satan. This image of the Christian life may well owe more to a common type of Christian biography than to the Bible. A surprising number of Christian biographies present an unrealistic and probably fanciful picture of how their subjects lived. They present Christian equivalents of Indiana Jones or Wonder Woman, whose exploits are 'spiritual' rather than death-defying feats in 'real life.' There is no doubt that this emphasis on the strong and triumphant individual has produced some outstanding people. It has however driven many more to a lonely struggle ending in despair and disillusionment, or to what is possibly worse, to the hypocrisy of a double-standard life. Here we struggle to maintain the omni-competent image in public and know ourselves to be something very different behind the scenes. The biblical ideal is something quite different. It presents what someone has called 'the omni-competent Christian fellowship', where the inclusive life of the communal body takes into account the weaknesses and limitations of each of us and complements these by the strengths of the whole.

The principle is unavoidably clear: we are not meant to carry our burdens alone. Certainly we can cast them on our Lord, but one of the ways he bears our weary burdens is through human fellowship and friendship. Paul, writing to the church in Corinth, beautifully illustrates this for us:

> For when we came into Macedonia, this body of ours had no rest, but we were harassed at every turn – conflicts on the outside, fears within. But God, who comforts the downcast, comforted us by the coming of Titus, and not only by his coming but also by the comfort you had given him. He told us about your longing for me, your deep sorrow, your ardent concern for me, so that my joy was greater than ever.[185]

Paul was worried to death about the believers in Corinth, but through the companionship of a friend he found strength. Thank goodness we do not have a typical Christian biography of Paul, but a real picture of him! How much more this encourages us, as we identify with his struggles.

Human friendship, in which we bear one another's burdens, is thoroughly part of the purpose of God for his people. By burden bearing, we fulfil the law of Christ. Instead of imposing the law as a burden on others, we should rather lift their burdens and so fulfil Jesus' law. Paul, in his weakness, found comfort in the strength of others.

We are now ready to see what restoration looks like in action. The letter to the Galatians raises the situation: 'If someone is caught in a sin.'[186] The phrase reminds us of the unnamed woman who was brought to Jesus by the Pharisees and accused of having been 'caught in the act of adultery.'[187] The Greek word for 'caught' means 'to overtake by surprise, to overpower before one can escape.' The expression used therefore can refer to either someone discovered to be sinning, or a person who has blundered into a period of unproductive living. It can mean obvious sin, deliberate wrongdoing, or a set of wrong choices that have knocked a someone off the path.

The Apostle in Galatians 5:26-6:2 has given us a set of guidelines for restoration.

What is to be done?

'Restore him'! The verb in Galatians 6:1 means 'to put in order' and so 'to restore to its former position.' In ordinary Greek usage, the word was a medical term for the setting of a fractured or dislocated bone. Mark also uses it of the disciples who were mending their nets – actually, cleaning, mending and folding them together in preparation for fishing.[188]

John Stott applies Paul's principle to church life today

Notice how positive Paul's instruction is. If we detect someone doing something wrong, we are not to stand by doing nothing on the pretext that it is none of our business and we have no wish to be involved. Nor are we to despise

or condemn him in our hearts and, if he suffers for his mis-
demeanour, say 'Serves him right' or 'Let him stew in his
own juice.' Nor are we to report him to the minister, or
gossip about him to our friends in the congregation. No, we
are to 'restore' him, to 'set him back on the right path.'[189]

This is how Martin Luther applied the command: 'Run
to him, and reaching out your hand, raise him up again,
comfort him with sweet words, and embrace him with
motherly arms.'[190]

Who is to get involved?

'You who are spiritual'![191] The Apostle has already
described spiritual people as those who are 'led by the
Spirit'; who 'keep in step with the Spirit'; so that 'the fruit
of the Spirit' appears in their lives.[192] Now all that kind of
language may appear a bit otherworldly and unreal. If this
is so, then the impression soon disappears when the
Apostle goes on to spell out how the spiritual works its way
out in practice. This is where the rubber of spirituality hits
the road of reality. Here Paul shows what it is like to be a
spiritual person – it is the one who takes the initiative in
lovingly restoring those who have gone off the rails.

This restorative action teaches us, among other things,
that true spirituality is not austere and uninviting. James
Philip, in his book *Christian Maturity*, puts a searching
question to us: 'Am I the kind of Christian that a man
who has failed would instinctively shrink from and say,
"Oh no, I could never confide in him" or would he feel
free to come to me in trouble?'[193]

Like a magnet, people who had failed felt drawn to
Jesus. His holiness seemed to attract them rather than
repel them! If we are not like him in attracting the broken

and defeated, then we need to ask ourselves why. It is possible to be energetically 'holy' and yet fearfully un-Christlike. If the Christian who has failed does not detect in us something of the compassion and sympathy of Christ – which is not the same as a weak toleration of sin and evil – then something has gone terribly wrong with our sanctification.

What is true of the individual also applies to our church fellowship. If it is not the kind of company where people who have failed feel welcomed and loved, the kind of place where we can face life again and begin to work our way back to the standards and patterns from which we have stumbled, then our church is denying the spirit of our Lord, no matter how orthodox its testimony.

How should we restore someone?

'Gently. But watch yourself.'[194] This is how Paul sets the tone of our approach to failure in others. Gentleness is part of the 'fruit of the Spirit.' And gentleness is linked to watchfulness. That suggests a gentleness that is born of a sense of our own weakness and proneness to sin.

Among the greatest and clearly unique gifts one Christian can give to another is to grant a restorative grace. Restoring grace can be just like a life belt thrown to a drowning person. Without it, rebuilding broken worlds is not possible. People not offered this grace litter society. Some made bad financial choices – and were left to get by as best they could, sometimes receiving practical help from their non-Christian friends to get them back on their feet. Others made bad moral choices – and were met with rejection, denied the fellowship of believers at the time they needed it most.

Why then do we talk about spiritual warfare and then show surprise when there are casualties? And why, when there are casualties, are we not more active in sending out the medics whose task it is to apply healing and restoring grace? The truth is that, if each of us knew how sinful we really are, our failures would not so shock or subdue us. Most of us, however, do not know the depths of our own depravity. Therefore, we are shocked, particularly by our fall into serious moral failure or by our surprising ability to deny Jesus Christ.

When we sin, it is one of the tactics of Satan to persuade us that, since we have lapsed, we have obviously forfeited our chance for a successful Christian life – we might as well go on sinning. The task of the restoring fellowship is to persuade us that is not all over for us spiritually and that we must leave our sins and come home to the Saviour.

There is no more beautiful example of restoring grace than that of Simon Peter. In the front rank of Jesus' followers, he failed big time! In the hour of Jesus' greatest need, he had not only abandoned him but had compounded his cowardice by a threefold denial that he had ever known the Master. 'I don't know what you're talking about … I don't know the man.'[195]

How does Jesus respond to his friend's open betrayal? To begin with, he prays for him. Unlike the disciples, Jesus knew Peter was going to deny him. He did not, however, give up on him, promising instead to pray for Peter. Prayer is not an addendum to our Christian love and service; it lies at the heart of it. It really is the most significant thing we can do for one another. This is why we must not promise to pray for someone unless we determine to do so!

Jesus also takes the initiative after the man's failure. When he appears to Mary, and sends through her his message to his disciples, he asks her to tell them 'and Peter' that he will see them in Galilee. Why does he mention Peter specifically? To signal to Peter that he still has time for him, that he is still concerned about him, and that he has not abandoned him. Is this the way we treat those who have failed, especially if their failure has hurt or embarrassed us? Do we feel instead that they should make all the moves?

Jesus, with great deliberation, allows the failed man to reaffirm his love and loyalty and then re-appoints him to service and fellowship. When Jesus and the disciples are reunited one morning on the lake shore of Galilee, he asks Peter three times if he loves him.[196] There is no doubt the repetition of the question must have hurt Peter's feelings. It would have brought back memories of the threefold denial. Was it cruel? It would have been cruel to let the denial fester, cruel to pretend it never happened, cruel to have let Peter go through the rest of his life feeling inferior and unworthy of his office. Peter had sinned publicly and therefore had to be restored publicly.

What about those who have abandoned the faith in some way? Should they be restored? Maybe they are denying truths they once held and pose a threat to the integrity of the gospel. Do we write such people off? Do we abandon them to their unbelief? Listen to these words of James, 'My brothers and sisters, if one of you should wander from the truth and someone should bring that person back, remember this: Those who turn sinners from the error of their ways will save them from death and cover over a multitude of sins.'[197] Here James draws a picture of a wilful turning away from the truth. James suggests that apart from outside help, such people will not find their way back to the path of spiritual growth. Someone needs to accept responsibility to win them back. It is not enough for us to say that others, not us, should do this. Whoever performs this rescue mission may, under God, save such a wayward believer 'from death, and cover over a multitude of sins.'

Mike: Restoring grace

Mike had been as successful as they come in the world of commerce. His company expanded rapidly and had been floated on the stock market. The profits came flowing in. The problem with this kind of success is that while crossing the globe chasing up the next customer, it is easy to overlook the details. An audit of his personal finances exposed tax evasion – Mike was arrested, tried and jailed. The publicity given to his case made a lot of his being active in his local church. The news media virtually camped outside the homes of church members demanding answers to headline questions.

There can be no doubt that many of his fellow Christians felt hurt, even betrayed, by Mike's fall from grace. He found himself not only having to cope with the indignities of prison life but also with the continual mockery of those who had heard of his Christian profession. In prison, his faith nearly gave way altogether. A mixture of wounded pride, shame and a sense of being an abject failure made him wonder whether he had been kidding himself all these years. What kept him going in prison, and what brought him back to the Lord in the end, was the stream of letters from church members and the visits from church leaders. This concern reaffirmed to him their love of him and their desire to welcome him back among them.

The leadership reported on their interview with Mike at his release at a memorable church meeting. Mike spoke in detail of his offences, wanting everyone to know not only that he was not keeping anything back from them but also that there was a heartfelt repentance on his part, as a result of God working in him. He also wanted to hold himself accountable to his brothers and sisters for his future behaviour. There was hardly a dry eye in the place and when, on the next Sunday, he was welcomed back into the fellowship there was much hugging and many smiles. Martin Luther said that 'the face of the church is the face of a sinner.' We shall never create a church that is without sin. One of the attractive hallmarks of a Christ-like local church, however, is the way in which it treats its wounded and fallen ones.

How do we know Mike's repentance is genuine? Should our acceptance of fellow believers who have fallen only take place after no possible doubt of their repentance remains? Have you done anything that, if taken further, could have publicly disgraced you? Imagine you are part of Mike's church. How would you explain the situation to someone outside the fellowship?

9

The meal of fellowship

Of all the events in which Christians participate, none has been a bigger source of contention than the celebration of the Lord's Supper, as it sometimes called. In fact, the varieties of description are indicative of the controversies that have surrounded this aspect of Christian worship. To some it is the sacrifice of the Mass in which the body of Christ is re-offered repeatedly on every altar in every duly consecrated church building. To others it is the Eucharist, which is the Greek word for 'thanksgiving.' For those who see themselves as recovering the simplicities of the gospel, it is the 'breaking of bread.'

Over the years, there has been the formalising of the Supper, to the extent that for many centuries it was kept at a physical distance from the people of God. When the reformers drew up their guidelines for the observance of the Supper in the Anglican Church, they envisaged the table in the centre of the nave, with the worshippers gathered all around it. As time passed, the table was moved eastwards, and then barricaded in. Now ordinary worshippers could not come near – a reversion to the old medieval errors.

Over history, there has also been the trivialising of the Supper. It is often now an option, sidelined into being a mere addendum of church life. The Supper has also been individualised. A strange and perverse idea has got around that the Lord's Supper is a flight of the alone to the Alone: it is *my communion I make*, not *our communion we share*. One cannot imagine a more radical denial of the Gospel than that. We have in fact just used perhaps one of the New Testament's most widely used words, 'communion', descriptive of what the Supper is, a word which challenges the divisiveness that surrounds the event. 'Communion' translates the expression that provides the focus of this book – *koinonia*. Whatever else the Lord's Supper is, it is an expression of our togetherness in Christ.

The link between fellowship, *koinonia*, and the Supper goes back to the two streams that run into our communion celebration.

First, there is the Passover meal. This was, for the Jews, an expression of their oneness within the life and destiny of the chosen people of God. The Passover was a community act in which the individual was gathered out of their personal isolation into a profound solidarity with the whole people of God.

Second, there is the Last Supper itself, which Jesus ate with his disciples the night before he died, which is itself the basis of the Lord's Supper. Here too, the corporate aspect comes to the surface, in two ways in particular. Jesus refers to the 'new covenant' in his blood. The entire covenant idea in the Old Testament is a profoundly corporate one. The covenant with Abraham gathers into its orbit the future generations of his descendants; this is why the reference to the 'new covenant' in Jeremiah chapter 31 addresses a corporate group or company of people. The ordinance of the Supper is then an act of the new covenant community; the new people of God. Picking this up on the eve of his death,[198] Jesus links the

Supper with the coming of the kingdom, in its two stages. In one, we now look back to the action by which the death and resurrection of Jesus establishes the kingdom. In another we look forward to its full manifestation, as we echo his words and repeat 'until he comes.'

The Supper as proclamation

The simplest and most obvious meaning of the Lord's Supper is that it commemorates the death of Jesus Christ on the Cross. The Apostle Paul put it like this: 'You proclaim the Lord's death until he comes.'[199] We remember his atonement as our substitute, most of all; it is this that the broken bread, representing the Lord's broken body, and the wine, representing his shed blood, most clearly signifies. Atonement has to do with our being made right with God – we are restored to being at one with him (at-one-ment). That the death was substitutionary means that this reconciliation was achieved by the sacrifice of another in our place.

Why did Jesus die? The Bible teaches that all who ever lived are sinners, having broken God's law, and that the penalty for sin is death. The Bible says, 'There is no one righteous, not even one; there is no one who understands, no one who seeks God. All have turned away, they have together become worthless; there is no one does good, not even one.'[200] It says, 'the soul who sins is the one who will die'[201] and 'the wages of sin is death.'[202] This death is not merely physical, though it is that. It is spiritual as well. Death is separation. Physical death is the separation of the soul and spirit from the body. Spiritual death is the separation of the soul/spirit from God. Eternal death is the separation of the soul, spirit and body from God forever. We deserve that separation as a consequence of our sin. Jesus, however, became our substitute by experiencing physical, spiritual and eternal death for us in our place on the cross. This is what happens during that dark period of four hours when the Son of God experienced God-forsakenness on the cross. Hell is God-forsakenness and on the cross, Jesus was forsaken in place of his people.

A vivid illustration of this principle of substitution and sacrifice is seen in the early chapters of Genesis. Adam and Eve had sinned and were in terror of the consequences. They knew God had warned them. He had said, 'You are free to eat from any every tree in the garden; but you must not eat from the tree of the knowledge of good and evil, for when you eat of it you will surely die.'[203] At that point they probably did not have a very clear idea of what death was, but they knew it was serious. Consequently, when they sinned through disobedience, and then later heard God walking toward them in the garden, they tried to hide.

No one of course can hide from God. God found them, called them out of hiding and began to deal with their transgression. What should we expect to happen as a result of that confrontation? Here is God, who told our first parents that in the day they sinned they would die. Here are Adam and Eve, who have sinned. In that situation, of course, we should expect the immediate execution of the sentence. If God had put them to death in that moment, physically, spiritually and eternally, banishing them from his presence forever, it would have been just.

That is not what happened. Instead we have God first rebuking the sin and then providing a sacrifice. He took an animal, killed it, and then used its skin to clothe them.[204] It was the first death anyone had ever witnessed and God enacted it! As Adam and Eve looked on, they must have been horrified. Yet even as they recoiled from the sacrifice, they must have marvelled as well. For what God was showing them was that, although they deserved to die, it was possible for another, in this case two animals, to die in their place. The animals paid the price of their sin, and they were clothed in the skins of the animals as a reminder of that fact.

That is the meaning of substitution. It is the death of one on behalf of another. Yet we must also say, as the Bible teaches, that the death of animals could never take away the penalty of sin. That event was only a symbol of how sin was to be taken away. Jesus Christ performed the real sacrifice, and we look back to it with awe and wonder in the communion service.

We also look back to something Jesus suggested when he spoke of the wine as 'the new covenant in my blood.' The cross was a victory on which God has established a new covenant of salvation with his redeemed people. A covenant is a solemn promise confirmed by an oath or a sign. So when Jesus speaks of the cup as commemorating a new covenant, he was pointing to the promises of salvation that God made to us on the basis of Christ's death. We look back to those promises with awe and wonder.

At the Last Supper the actions of his hands and the words of his mouth combined to speak of his death. The bread and wine symbolise his body and blood. Moreover, the body and blood signify not Christ's life, but his death. His loving purpose is that we should share at the Lord's Table not in his life and its power, but in his death and its benefits. The Supper presents him as our crucified Saviour, who laid down his life for our forgiveness. Eating and drinking are the visible and physical equivalents of the invisible and spiritual reality of believing and receiving by faith all that he has accomplished for us. Faith is a personal reaching out of the heart to Jesus, and a personal laying hold on him, to be our Saviour and Lord. Looking back to the benefits of his death, and how accessible they are by faith, fills us with awe and wonder.

The Supper as participation

In his letter to the church in Corinth, the Apostle Paul asserts that to share in the Lord's Supper involves a 'participation' [*koinonia*] in the body and blood of Christ.

> Is not the cup of thanksgiving for which we give thanks a participation in the blood of Christ? And is not the bread that we break a participation in the body of Christ? Because there is one loaf, we, who are many, are one body, for we all partake of the one loaf.[205]

We enter into the experience of the cross, the ground of our salvation, very much as the Jewish believer was enabled, by the Passover, to relive the experience of those who came out of bondage in Egypt. The Lord's Supper, then, is more than a simple act of remembrance, a sort of Christian Poppy Day, in which we recall the giving of life on our behalf and the cost of our freedom. It is that of course; as Jesus said, 'Do this in remembrance of me.'[206] It is more, however, than that. It is also a point of fellowship with the risen and exalted Lord. Where there is a living faith, a blessing derives from taking part. When we approach the Supper in faith, we see portrayed in vivid symbol the costly act of sacrifice which atoned for our sin, and there we meet again our blessed Lord and taste again the benefits of his suffering. There we feed on him by faith, in the Spirit, and are gathered into communion with him in his ascended glory. We meet him at his table. He is the host and we are his guests; we experience God's hospitality. Here, as someone said, 'pardoned sinners sit and hold communion with their Lord.' The Lord's Supper is not a sacrifice of Christ. We do not offer Christ to God in it. Rather, we remember Christ's sacrifice; we enjoy the relationship with him it made possible – we do not in any sense repeat it or re-present it. If there is any sacrifice at the Supper table, it is the sacrifice of ourselves. We bring our bodies, our gifts and our praises and give them up to him who gave himself for us.

The Lord's Supper also involves our participation in the lives of other Jesus people. Many times in 1 Corinthians 11 Paul uses the verb 'to meet' or 'to come together.' The Lord's Supper is a gathering together of Christian people. In the passage quoted above we have the image of those who are eating being 'one loaf.' The single loaf, which was broken and shared by all, spoke clearly of the single life, which all partakers shared in that one Lord. The loaf also points us to the 'body of Christ' which again has a twofold reference. It refers to the physical 'body' of Jesus sacrificed on the cross but it also refers to the Church which is the 'Body of Christ' on earth. So the whole imagery of the Supper has this application of community as well as a salvation.

The Supper as our examiner

In chapter 11 Paul deals with certain abuses of the Supper: divisions (verse 18) and self-centredness (verse 21). Paul sees this unworthy behaviour as despising the church of God (verse 22) and sharply rebukes those who are guilty of this. With such abuses going on as they gathered, there could be no genuine celebration of the Supper (verse 20).

In other words, for Paul there could be no real sharing in the Lord's Supper where there was no genuine oneness of spirit and behaviour among those taking part. Where the celebration does not flow out of real unity among the participants, the Supper is profaned. In those days, in the first century, communion was most often celebrated informally at the end of a shared meal together, or at some other social event. The implication of this is clear; a group of people who cannot eat a meal together or talk over a cup of coffee with genuine warmth of friendship cannot really appreciate what they are doing when they eat the Lord's Supper together. This probably calls into question our normal practice of communion, that is, participating in large scale, impersonal settings rather than in the quiet informality of a small and intimate group.

Andrew Murray put the issue clearly: 'How often have the guests at Jesus' table sat next to one another for years in succession without knowing or loving one another or helping one another. Many a one has sought after closer communion with the Lord and not found it, because he would have the Head alone without the Body. Would that it were thoroughly understood – Jesus must be loved, and honoured, and served and known in His members.'[207] In other words, we cannot have the head without the body. We cannot expect to grow in our relationship with him if we are consistently careless of our relationships with his people.

In 1 Corinthians 11 we are encouraged to 'examine' ourselves before participating (verse 28). In a Jewish home on Passover night the house was hunted and searched for any trace of leaven. Leaven, or yeast, is often regarded as a symbol of evil in the Scriptures, because it is always swelling and seething up. We read earlier in the letter, 'Get rid of the old yeast that you may be a new batch without yeast.'[208] We should not eat a regular meal without washing our hands first. Similarly, no one should take the Supper of the Lord without first self-examination, repentance and cleansing. Repentance must be real. It is no good my repenting of cruel gossip or seething resentment if I intend to keep it up. The Ten Commandments and the Sermon on the Mount, along with our own known weaknesses, form a valuable check-list for this useful, if uncomfortable, expedient of self-examination.

The context of Paul's words, however, suggests that the main area for self-examination should be our relationship with those who sit around us in the congregation! Jesus speaks of leaving our offering at the altar and first being reconciled to a brother or sister.[209] The order is significant: first go, then come! It is a call to be sensitive to sin, especially in the form of hurt to others. It is a call to be responsive to conscience – when it comes to mind, go immediately and do something about it. We must not allow an estrangement to remain, still less to grow.

If we have sinned against our neighbour, we must confess our sin to them and ask for forgiveness. Here is the picture. I am at the Lord's Table. A person walks in and sits down. I am reminded of an incident, an event; some words spoken in haste. Perhaps I can think of no reason at all for the fact that that brother or sister has a grievance against me. It is no use going on with the service once that thought has come to mind. We cannot draw near to God while we are distanced from another. I may need to slip over to someone and ask for forgiveness before I can carry on. The Lord's Table calls for this kind of action.

God's purpose for his people, as revealed in his Word, is that we should live in harmony with himself and with each other. We are called to peace.[210] We are to 'seek peace and pursue it.'[211] Christianity is in essence a religion of peace and reconciliation. Therefore, we must take seriously every situation in which fellowship is marred or broken. We must make it our aim to live at peace with everyone.

Darija: Experiencing a form of words – the surface and the reality

The Lord's Supper, as a supreme example of God's hospitality, has parallels in the meal-time, whether in a family or a social context.

The Big Issue magazine recounted the true story of Darija, who is a lawyer from Sarajevo who came to Britain for refuge during the last Balkan war. She was initially delighted to be invited for a meal by a well-off and elegant housewife. She was quickly humiliated by her hostess's patronising attitude and unfeeling questions. Darija realised that, for her hostess, having a refugee for a meal was merely a tool for gaining prestige with her friends. Her alienation was all too soon made apparent:

> I entered the most beautiful dining room I have ever seen. Everything was perfect, from the stunning interior to the crockery, cutlery, the glasses on the table, and of course, the remarkable guests. All of them rich, with a perfect image; chatty, full of self-confidence.

> I was the only one who was not perfect. I was heartbroken, financially broken, dressed from a charity shop, feeling so uncomfortable, wanting to run away. But how could I? I was a special guest, although I felt more like the main course, invited to dinner as a great honour to show me

– and to prove to each other – how much they cared for me.
Did they?[212]

Darija recounts how her hostess then whispered a question – was she all right with a knife and fork? She managed to reply that she would try not to cut herself. She was then asked if she had gone to school 'down there' (i.e. in Bosnia). She simply replied in the affirmative, and that she was a lawyer.

This act of apparent kindness and hospitality came over as cold and intimidating to the refugee, new to England. How can our celebration of the Lord's Supper create barriers with fellow believers, instead of reflecting God's warm hospitality? What can we do for the Supper to be a true proclamation in which we truly participate as believers together in fellowship and communion? What is the proper focus for our self-examination? Imagine someone like Darija (assuming that she was a believer) attending the Lord's Supper in your church. Would she feel at home, or alienated?

10

Growing together in groups

When Jesus came, he preached to the masses the kingdom of God. He gathered around him about five hundred disciples to whom he gave teaching that was more intensive. But it was to the twelve that he devoted most of his time and among whom he found the closest fellowship. Even from this close group, he chose to relate more closely with Peter, James and John.

In his book *Body Life*, Ray Stedman observes that 'the early church relied upon a twofold witness as a means of reaching and impressing a cynical and unbelieving world, *kerygma* (that is, proclamation) and *koinonia* (that is, fellowship).'[213] It was the combination of these two, which made their witness so powerful and effective. Contemporary pagans could easily shrug off the proclamation as simply another teaching among many; but they found it much more difficult to reject the evidence of *koinonia*. The concern of Christians for each other, and their evident awareness of sharing in the same great family of God as brothers and sisters, left the pagan world of their day drooling with envy.

We shall always need *kerygma* and *koinonia*, proclamation and fellowship. However, while it may be hard to find genuine proclamation in the twenty-first century

West, it is also hard to find authentic fellowship. If the answer to recovering authentic Christian proclamation is the rehabilitation of biblical preaching, then the answer to recovering genuine Christian fellowship is the restoration of small groups. What are the arguments for growing together through groups?

What the Bible shows us

On the first Christian Sunday, after the Spirit fell at the Feast of Pentecost, the church in Jerusalem numbered over three thousand people. Within months this group is likely to have swollen to well over ten thousand people. Acts chapter 2 tells us how such a large group operated – 'they continued to meet together in the Temple courts,' presumably the only space big enough to accommodate such numbers, and in their homes. It was in each other's homes that they ate meals together and responded to one another's needs. It was in that context of meeting in houses that they saw the Lord add to their numbers daily 'those who were being saved.'

The New Testament contains injunctions about how we should relate to each other within the body of Christ.[214] Many of these call for a more intimate setting than our formal church services. Many people attend church on a Sunday looking for a 'fellowship' where they can be known and loved, only to walk away disillusioned that they have not found it. However, of course, the problem is that they are looking for it in the wrong place. We gather on Sunday in order to offer corporate worship to God, to sit under the authority of his Word, and to witness to the world that we are a people who belong together under the authority of God himself. Numbers are irrelevant. We can do this with two people or with twenty thousand; in some respects, the more the merrier! However, you cannot have fellowship with more than twenty people. In fact, the ideal group with which to have a meaningful relationship is probably between eight and twelve.

What history shows us

Throughout the history of the church, there has been this recognition of the need for smaller groups if we are to grow together in fellowship.

The English Reformation finds its roots in a small group of men, including Robert Barnes and Matthew Parker, who met in the White Horse Inn in Cambridge to study the Greek New Testament of Erasmus. Another influential group was called the Clapham Sect. These were a few social reformers, active near the end of the eighteenth century and into the nineteenth. They got their name because they met in the home in Clapham, London, of Henry Thornton and William Wilberforce (who was famous for his achievement of abolishing slavery worldwide). Most of the members were evangelical Anglicans and members of Parliament. Known as the 'Saints,' they not only worked for the abolition of the slave trade and slavery, but also to improve prison conditions and the working conditions of labourers. They also helped to start several missionary societies, including the British and Foreign Bible Society and the Church Missionary Society. In our own time, another small group has been influential in communicating Christian faith in a modern world shaped by the media. This was an informal club of literary friends who met weekly in a tiny Oxford pub, and included J.R.R. Tolkien, (whose readers in a poll voted his Christian fantasy, *The Lord of the Rings*, 'Book of the Century'), C.S. Lewis and Charles Williams. One of their concerns was to write stories that would have a wide appeal in a post-Christian world.

Luther grew to recognise the importance of an inner core of believers in the church, and their need for a more intimate and devout fellowship. In his Preface to *The German Mass and Order of Service*, Luther identified three kinds of worship: the Latin Mass; the German liturgy; and a third, which he describes as a church within the church.

> These two orders of service must be used publicly, in the churches, for all the people, among whom are many who do not believe and are not yet Christians...That is not yet a well-ordered and organised congregation in which Christians could be ruled according to the gospel....
>
> The third kind of service should be a truly evangelical order and should not be held in a public place for all sorts of people. But those who want to be Christians in earnest and who profess the gospel with hand and mouth should sign their names and meet alone in a house somewhere to pray, to read, to baptise, to receive the sacrament, and to do other Christian works....Here one could set up a brief and neat order for baptism and the sacrament and centre everything on the Word, prayer and love.[215]

The principle of change through the small group can be seen in the Methodist movement. Its real starting point lay in the conversion of the Wesleys, John and Charles, and their friend George Whitefield. They were part of a small group, which met in Oxford early in the eighteenth century to read literature and encourage personal piety. They also visited the sick and people in prison. They were nicknamed 'the Holy Club' by fellow students.

Following his conversion, John Wesley set out 'to reform the nation, particularly the church, and to spread scriptural holiness over the land.'[216] The phenomenal number of new converts raised a pastoral problem of conserving the fruits of the revival. The starting point in the growth of Methodist organisation was the fundamental Christian need for fellowship. This Wesley regarded as the most serious deficiency in the established Church of his day. 'Look east, west, north and south, name what parish you please, is Christian fellowship there? Rather, are not the bulk of the parishioners a mere rope of sand? What Christian connection is there between them? What intercourse in spiritual things? What watching over each other's souls?'[217]

The basic unit in Methodism was 'the society', which we might describe as a local church. This was broken down into classes or bands. These met weekly in groups of no more than four or five for the purpose of sharing Christian experience and telling each other's faults 'and that plain and home.'[218] They were responsible for the expulsion of members. Their discussion was strictly secret: hence 'in band' in Methodist parlance is the equivalent of 'in camera.' It was the establishment of this 'class' system within Methodism that served to conserve the converts reached through the ministry of John Wesley.

In Wales the 'Experience meeting' was a similar concept encouraged by the other great evangelist of that Great Awakening of the eighteenth century, George Whitefield. He wrote,

My brethren let us plainly and freely tell one another what God has done for our souls. To this end you would do well, as others have done, to form yourselves into little companies of four or five each, and meet once a week to tell each other what is on your hearts; that you may also pray for and comfort each other as need shall require. None but those who have experienced it can tell the unspeakable advantages of such a union and communion of souls. None I think that truly loves his own soul and his brethren as himself, will shy of opening his heart, in order to have their advice, reproof, admonition and prayers, as occasions require. A sincere person will esteem it one of the greatest blessings.

Korea's 'cell church'

The largest single local church in the history of Christianity exists, as I write, in Korea. It is the Yoido Full Gospel Church in Seoul. It has grown from five people who gathered in a tent in 1958, to a congregation of over 600,000 in 1989. After spurts of growth using more traditional church methods, Dr. Cho instituted cell groups in 1964. In the first five years, without cell groups, the congregation grew to about 3,800 people. By September, 1980, however, the congregation had 141,000 members. In the nine years to 1989 the church has averaged a growth of 140 members every single day!

Today dozens of other churches are using the cell church pattern, and all are growing at an amazing rate in Seoul. The world's two largest Presbyterian churches, along with the largest Methodist church, are cell group congregations. All are multiplying at a rate which far outstrips sister Korean churches who do not take advantage of a cell group structure.[219]

What pastoring shows us

In every congregation there is a need for better and more personal pastoral oversight. The fact that no one can adequately pastor more than ten people raises a question about the traditional role of the minister. The gift of pastoring must obviously be more widespread than individual ministers; the responsibility for pastoring falls on us all. *Episcope*, or oversight, is not the job only of a few; it is entrusted to all of us. The letter to the Hebrews tells us, 'See to it [episkopountes] that no one misses the grace of God.'[220] We are, each of us, our brother's and sister's keeper. We all need to learn to pastor each other.

John Wesley found this need of pastoring. On April 25th 1742 he recorded in his journal:

> I appointed several earnest and sensible men to meet me, to whom I showed the great difficulty I had long found of knowing the people who desired to be under my care. After much discourse, they all agreed there could be no better way to come to a sure, thorough knowledge of each person than to divide them into classes, like those in Bristol, under the inspection of those in whom I could most confide. This was the origin of our classes at London, for which I can never sufficiently praise God, the unspeakable usefulness of the institution having ever since been more and more manifest.

Nurture

The first small groups in the New Testament 'committed themselves to the Apostles' teaching.' They studied and submitted themselves to the Word of God. They allowed his living Word to nurture them.

Worship

The first Christian small group 'praised God with glad and sincere hearts.' Praise involves consciously giving God the glory due to his name. Praise is backed up by a constant habit of proper thankfulness to God that gives health and a glow to our lives.

Community

The first Christians developed their common life together. Such communality will happen both in a religious context and in a social context. It involves getting to know each other; developing open lines of communication with each other; learning to accept and enjoy diversity in the group; and caring for individual needs.

Mission

The first Christians were committed to getting the gospel out. They did it in the most natural of settings, in the marketplace and in their homes. We truly find ourselves when we are the representatives of Christ in our place of business, and in the neighbourhoods where we live. We have never properly exploited the opportunities both afford to make an impact of the gospel.

Sometimes small groups meet for specific tasks. A group may be responsible for running a social action project, a finance team, or the music ministry in a church. There can be an infinite variety of small groups in any local church. Whatever the specific role of the group, however, these key pastoral ingredients of mission, community, worship, and nurture must be nourished if the group is to be truly Christian and if it is to make a vital impact on the world.

Some practical considerations

What are the advantages of small groups in developing fellowship?

1. Small groups are flexible

They can change their procedures and functions to meet changing situations or to accomplish different objectives. Because of their informality they have little need for rigid patterns of operation. They are free to be flexible as to place, time, frequency and length of their meetings.

2. Small groups are mobile

They can meet in a home, office, or shop, anywhere. They can go where the people are and do not have to rely on persuading strangers to enter a foreign environment.

3. Small groups are inclusive

They can demonstrate an openness to outsiders that is winsome and attractive. The small group is open to all types of people. As Elton Trueblood says, 'When a person is drawn into a little circle, devoted to prayer and to deep sharing of spiritual resources, he is well aware he is welcomed for his own sake, since the small group has no budget, no officers concerned with the success of their administration, and nothing to promote.' Because they are inclusive, you are missed if you do not come. You could miss the average church for months and your absence not be noticed!

4. Small groups are personal

Christian communication can sometimes appear too slick, professional and impersonal. In a small group, communication takes place at a personal level. The small group may reach more people effectively than the mass media. They create a place that meets my needs and the needs of those others who commit themselves to it.

5. *Small groups can grow by division*

A small group is effective only when small. When a group reaches critical mass, numbers will start to decline unless there is division. Small groups divide in order to multiply. There are endless possibilities for numerical growth without large financial outlays or diluting spiritual impact.

6. *Small groups are an effective means of evangelism*

A small group can often be the best introduction to Christianity for our unchurched friends. A night out together for some fun, a meal together, a book evening; the possibilities are endless.

Josh Moody says, 'We will win the world when we realise that fellowship, not evangelism, must be our primary emphasis. When we demonstrate the Big Miracle of Love, it won't be necessary for us to go out – they will come in.' I am not sure about Moody's need to have fellowship without evangelism, but this emphasis may be necessary to redress the imbalance where we focus on evangelistic events and neglect the pursuing of biblical fellowship.

7. Small groups help develop leadership

Not all Christian leadership is meant to be 'up-front.' However, biblical leadership does mean 'taking people on in their relationship with God.' Leaders have to emerge somewhere in the life of the church, and the small group is the ideal setting for identifying such a gift and a calling in areas like pastoring, serving, teaching and evangelism.

Small groups, then, should not be an adjunct to church life; we need to see them as a vital and primary expression of the church's life together. George Webber observes: 'These are the two foci of our life as Christians. … We join in congregational worship. We meet in small groups.'

Janie: Growing pains

Janie is a Head of Department in a large secondary school. She is often tired, working many evenings and much of her holidays to administer her job conscientiously. Classes in her subject have improved considerably since she took over, despite behaviour problems with students in the school. It serves a large housing estate with many social problems.

For several years, since starting to attend the church, Janie has preferred to take a quiet role. She has never volunteered to help in the Sunday Club, or in the midweek meeting for under fourteens. She attends her home-group most weeks, however, and contributes enthusiastically to the discussions.

What gifts does Janie have that could benefit the life of the church? Should she be encouraged to take a more active role? If so, how could she participate more without burning out?

11

Friends

Of all the popular TV shows among young people in the early part of this new millennium, none is as popular as that of a groups of twenty-something friends in a New York apartment building. The world is looking for friendships. Friends that can be trusted to stick with you through thick and thin. Films like *Notting Hill* point us to the value of a group of true friends who accept us as we are.

Building friendships is a vital part of our Christian and human growth. Friends stabilise us; they support us in times of struggle; they prick the bubble of our egos and keep our feet on the ground. Jesus needed friends and so do we. Friendships go beyond a dinner party or office acquaintances that often pass as friendships in our urban society.

How do we relate to God, to our children, to our spouse, and to our friends? Most of us – let's admit it – have superficial relationships. Yet relationships are what people are looking for. Often we try to short circuit relationship building and opt for a shared activity like football or shopping as an alternative to the much more costly work of building a relationship with someone. The Bible urges us to make friends. Be sure to marry one of your friends if you get married at all.

I had occasion to speak recently to the mother of someone who was converted a few years ago. This woman did her utmost to prove to me that her daughter was somehow mentally ill since she had come to faith. She told me how before becoming a Christian her daughter would bring her boyfriends home and they would sleep together, 'a perfectly natural thing to do', the mother said. When she brought a Christian guy home, however, they stayed in different rooms, refusing to sleep together till they were married. This mother took that to be a sign of something fundamentally wrong in the relationship between her daughter and the man who is now her son-in-law. Perhaps you know what it is like for your family to reject you. If so, you need to make new friends in Christ – these friendships could potentially be closer than that of family members.

Beginning friendships

Conversation often begins over food or in a situation where you are thrown together with someone for a prolonged period. Your train might halt for an hour while the track ahead is inspected. Usually conversation starts slowly as we talk about what we like and dislike, where we come from, common interests and the like. Conversation will dry up if we are judgemental in our attitudes or if we are critical of the other person's views, culture, clothes or whatever. Usually, unless our new friend is a Christian, talk about faith will not happen until we are well into our relationship with them.

Parents should talk to their children naturally about truth as issues arise. As you read the Old Testament, you find parents being told to be ready to respond to questions as they are asked: 'What do these stones mean'?

(about the stone memorial at the Jordan); or 'How is this night different from other nights'? (about the Passover ritual). Bedside chats as children are settled for the night can be one of the most meaningful contexts in which to discuss issues. They can be the key to developing meaningful friendships between parents and children.

Communication will, of course, take time. It may mean not turning the light out immediately you get into bed with your spouse at night. It may very well be that you are exhausted but that your husband or wife is ready to talk. It may mean missing your favourite TV programme as you listen for the umpteenth time to the day's story from your little child. It may mean not having that game of golf this week or foregoing watching that football match. Most of us are selfish creatures and that demanding self has to be denied in order to build relationships. We need to learn to linger over others. This, not surprisingly, is also true of our relationship with God. We need to meditate on his truth. When we are ready to let time to communicate eat into our schedule we shall know the joy of relating at a deeper level. It is worth the sacrifice.

Those who are married have to be intent on making time to communicate. It will not happen otherwise. There are so many things to do, and the children take up so much energy, especially from their mother. Parents need to plan times when they can talk together and keep to these times. However much two people love each other, they cannot remain best friends unless they communicate in an extended way. Couples are meant to be friends.

The kind of impression the media and office gossip gives about meeting and falling in love tends to be sex- and bed-oriented. 'Falling in love' is a highly charged business, there is no doubt. We need this emotional charge if we are ever going to make an effort to reach out to the person we are meant to marry. Nevertheless, being turned on is not the only criteria. For one thing, you may fall in love more than once in your life. So how do you know which one to marry? Do you marry them all? The key to knowing whom to marry is to understand that 'in-love-ness' is only one part of it. Do you respect the person? Do you respect their views? Do you want to talk to them, to share your secrets with them? In short, you should marry the friend who also sends you sky-high! The rush of sexual energy will cool down, but where there is real and mutual communication, the relationship will last until you are parted by death.

Care with friendships

We live in a fallen world, which means that as sinners we can easily foul up our relationships. Therefore, we have to care for and nurture them. I learned one of the dangers from my mother. While at college I had come to know a newly married couple. Stewart and I had a lot in common and we spent a lot of time talking about those things. My mother gave me this verse from Proverbs 25:17, 'Seldom set foot in your neighbour's house – too much of you, and you will be hated.' What is that proverb saying? Don't make a pest of yourself. Be sensitive. If your friend is busy, don't stay too long. If you are visiting a friend at home and her husband comes home after a day's work, excuse yourself and give them time together. Some of us exasperate our friends because we impose on their private spaces. We can make this mistake with the people we live with. Did you know that your wife and your children need their own space too? They are not there just to please you when you feel like it.

Friendships can go wrong in many ways. Adultery is a sinful form of friendship. There are warnings to keep away from situations that could make you open to temptation. These need heeding. I say this carefully: sex can seriously damage your friendships. What happens in premature sex is that you get ahead of yourself – you show disrespect for the person you involve as well as expressing disobedience to God.

Possessiveness also can destroy a good friendship. Maybe you are going out with someone and you resent the friends they had before you met. Maybe you are married and you expect your spouse to find all their needs met by you alone. You may be the kind of person who gives a wife or husband a hard time for wanting to see old friends or make new ones. If so, you are being just plain awkward, and you are making your relationship claustrophobic.

Commitment to friendships

In proper friendship we are talking of relationships where people 'stick' to each other. This might be our relationship to God, to our spouse, to our children or to our friends. In modern language, this means commitment. Relationships are vulnerable.

Selfishness undermines relationships. The Bible has much to say about selfish relationships. Proverbs 14:20 observes, 'The poor are shunned even by their neighbours, but the rich have many friends.' Another proverb (chapter 19:4) says something very similar, 'Wealth brings many friends, but the friends of the poor desert them.' On the same theme a proverb warns (19:6), 'Many curry favour with a ruler, and everyone is the friend of one who gives gifts.' These verses condemn people who are in friendships for what they can get out of them. The rich, the influential, the caring, the person who is a bundle of laughs, all will often attract friends like flies. They attract people who are social climbers, or those who want their needs met. In other words, it is all too easy for our relationships to be selfish. Our commitment in these cases is to what someone can do for us, not to the person.

Steadfastness, by contrast, strengthens relationships. There is an Old Testament word, which the NIV translates as 'unfailing love.' Others translate it as 'loyalty.' The idea is that just as God remains faithful to his covenant with Israel, whatever the situation may be, so must we be faithful to our friends.

One of the Proverbs tells us, 'Like a bad tooth or a lame foot is reliance on the unfaithful in times of trouble.'[221] The name for a friend who is not there for us in our time of trouble is 'unfaithful.' One of the saddest instances of this is described by the Apostle Paul, 'At my first defence, no one came to my support, but everyone deserted me.'[222] Here he was on trial for the gospel, and the Christians did not want to know him. Why do we forsake people in their time of trouble?

Firstly, we are ashamed of associating with people who are down. You can see this in the workplace. Someone you are friendly with starts going through a rough time; to be seen to be associated with them might threaten your job prospects, so you back off. It happens in churches, also. The pastor is called to go to another church. In the weeks before his departure, people who were close to him start pulling back as they realise a new leader is coming. They re-position themselves so they are not too closely identified with the old regime. Jim Bakker was a TV evangelist who dramatically fell and brought disgrace to the cause of Christ. How should Christians respond? Keep him at a distance? Members of Billy

Graham's family visited him in prison. God broke that man and brought him to a deep repentance, and friends kept him from sinking into despair while that process was going on.

Secondly, we distance ourselves from those in trouble because we have no time to get involved. Perhaps a friend is depressed or distressed by some life circumstances. To hear them properly and support them would take time, so we pull back. How many husbands do not take the time to sit and listen to their wives or to explain carefully what is going on in their lives, as they would to a colleague at work? You have heard the old chestnut, 'my wife does not understand me.' Often that is the case because we have not worked hard enough at explaining where we are. For us, as Christians, a priority should be the needs of our friends. We must make time for them.

The principle of commitment in friendship can be applied to marriage. Are we committed to our marriages? Commitment gives security upon which you can build romance. Christian love is a fundamental commitment to another person. In our friendships this love means a lasting allegiance to someone, a seeking of their greater good; in our marriages it means a daily determination to making the union work. 'Incompatibility' is an in-word, often cited as a reason for the break-up of a marriage. However, I have yet to meet two people who are totally compatible. The question to ask yourself is, are you in the relationship just to please yourself? When self-fulfilment is defined in such a way as to preclude personal suffering, then incompatibility, of course, becomes grounds for divorce. But there is a better way. Commitment in friendship and in marriage gives us the strength to face up to problems and work towards their solution. Many couples find that after numerous stormy and painful years, God's grace finally wins through and a joyful relationship emerges. Others have not seen such resolution, because one partner has been inflexible. Then the other partner chooses the path of suffering and refuses to give up trying to find a resolution. They have a whole eternity to enjoy the rewards of such faithfulness in heaven. When relationships get tough we need to take the long-term approach and remember that what we are doing counts for eternity. Beware then of the philosophy that offers short-term pleasure or fulfilment without commitment. When trouble comes, then you see who your friends are. Another proverb points out: 'Do not forsake your friend and the friend of your parent, and do not go to your relative's house when disaster strikes you – better a neighbour nearby than a relative far away.'[223] Some people have a romantic idea of what a natural family should be like, and are disappointed when their relatives do not measure up to this impossible ideal. Others who have no natural family ache within, feeling that they are missing out. This verse tells us to keep up our friendships because friends will be the ones to help us when we are in trouble.

Sometimes, of course, we shy away from committing ourselves to a relationship because we are afraid of failure, of showing weakness, or of being rejected. There are some who will not take the plunge and get married, when they should for the sake of the other. Real relationships involve risk. Couples I know have been going together for what seems like forever but one of them is scared to take the plunge. Either they should throw in the relationship (after all, they are not getting any younger) or they should just go for it. The alternative is to take our fragile egos and wrap them up in little hobbies, in habits and activities that keep others at a distance. That way our hearts will never get broken, but will become hard, unbreakable. The only guarantee that

you will be free of a broken heart is never to love anyone
or anything, not even a pet or a car!

Counsel – the way to mature friendship

The book of Proverbs offers us these pieces of wisdom:
'Plans fail for lack of counsel, but with many advisors
they succeed,' and 'Make plans by seeking advice; if you
wage war, obtain guidance.'[224] Can you see the point of
this advice? Our emotions can affect our perspective on
issues. They colour the very way that we see life.

Our selfishness, particularly, can affect our judgements. Some of our acquaintances affirm our egos. They
hang on to our every word. They frequently compliment
us and we feel comfortable around them. In an ancient
myth Narcissus looks in to a pool and falls in love with
his own reflected image. Narcissism, as it is called, is a
feature of our day, a special temptation. We seek for the
comfort of our reflection in others. Pouring cold water
on this attitude, the wise person says, 'The way of fools
seem right to them, but the wise listen to advice... Listen
to advice and accept instruction, and in the end you will
be wise.'[225]

Sometimes friendship involves wounding or being
wounded. Proverbs says, 'Better is open rebuke than
hidden love. Wounds from a friend can be trusted, but an
enemy multiplies kisses.'[226] Friends must wound us
sometimes because they love us. This happens when
they observe our weaknesses and errors. Sometimes we
pull back from friends because they have been honest
with us. Sometimes we hold our tongues because we are
afraid to risk the friendship.

'Whoever listens to a life-giving rebuke will be at home
among the wise,' runs the proverb. 'Those who ignore

discipline despise themselves, but those who heed correction gain understanding.'[227] We need visionaries in the kingdom of God, but we also need advisors. I am grateful for those who have saved me from a lot of trouble because they have intervened with good advice. I often thought they were boring and lacked vision, but they have proved to be right. Some of us are not very teachable because we try to project an image that we are mature or learned. We build a wall around ourselves and our minds are difficult to penetrate – especially when it comes to talking about our faults. The Bible has much to say about the value of soft hearts that God's Spirit – and fellow Christians who are the agents of the Spirit – can easily penetrate.

Giving comfort in friendship

The quality of friendship we have been describing is open to those who know God's love through Jesus Christ. Much of what we have said applies in marriage, in family life and among Christian friends. One key element, which is the most beautiful of all, is the comfort we are able to give one another.

Comfort when we offend

A proverb points out the difference between covering over a painful matter and repeating it: 'Whoever covers over an offence promotes love, but whoever repeats the matter separates close friends.'[228] Repeating the matter is the very opposite of covering a sin. To repeat a matter is to harp on about it, bringing it up repeatedly. It also includes talking about it to others. This is how the Bible understands forgiveness: once a person has confessed a sin and been forgiven, God does not remember that sin any more.[229] Before a sin can be forgiven, the wrongdoer must acknowledge it and take responsibility for it. This is where some of our relationships break down. Without this acceptance of guilt, there can be no forgiveness and no real fellowship either.[230] Once a sin is confessed, however, there can be forgiveness – and a determination to put it into the past and to move on. Too many of us, especially in marriage, do not let go of past sins and hurts, even after they have been faced up to by the offender. Is there someone you need to apologise to for not letting go of x from the past, and to affirm that you want to move forward together, by God's grace, and to leave x behind?

Comfort when we fall

We are not very good at handling failure, either our own or that of others. 'Two are better than one... If they fall down, one can help the other up,' we are told. 'But pity those who fall and have no friend to help them up.'[231] Failure can make us over-discouraged. Friends can help us regain sufficient courage to try again. They can also act as an accountability group – two or three people to whom we hold ourselves accountable for actions and for the consequences of decisions we make. Within marriage, accountability is a healthy feature that needs careful nurturing. When we get threatened by the questions of our spouse the likelihood is that we have something to hide! It is a great liberation actively to encourage an openness to each other where naturally and without undue prying, life becomes an open book. It is also the way of safety. For if I have made it my habit to tell my spouse precisely what has gone on in the office today, then it will be harder for me to play those mind games that can lead to unfaithfulness and failure.

Comfort in times of need

'If two lie down together, they will keep warm. But how can one keep warm alone?' the writer of Ecclesiastes asks.[232] Travellers would sleep close together to keep warm. The principle is that when we are battered by circumstances, criticisms, or disappointments, we need to find warmth somewhere. We need relationships of warmth. 'Though one may be overpowered, two can defend themselves,' the writer continues.[233] We need people who will be a friend to us in our need, and not leave us to our own devices, where we will be overpowered by fear or circumstance. This lack of friendship in time of need can happen within marriage. We expect our partner to work out a problem on their own as quickly as possible. How dare they expect us to sit down and do the hard work of prising out of them what is really wrong? Yet, for Christians, the needs of our friends should be a top priority. This care for others is what won the pagan world of the first centuries. 'See how these Christians love one another,' they said. The best way to show you love someone (to state the obvious) is not to send them a soppy card or to give them a warm hug, though these can be good reminders. It is, rather, to give someone your most valuable commodity, your time. Perhaps we spread ourselves too thinly; we have many acquaintances but few friends to whom we are truly committed.

As the proverb says, 'A friend loves at all times, and a relative is born for adversity.'[234] Friends are not just for fair weather, but for better for worse; for richer for poorer; in sickness and in health. Friendship is the bedrock of fellowship and community, at the heart of the *koinonia* of the king. As Jesus said, 'My command is this: Love each other as I have loved you. Greater love has no one than this, to lay down one's life for one's friends. … I no longer call you servants, because servants do not know their master's business. Instead, I have called you friends.'[235]

William and John: Friendship through thick and thin

William studied law many years ago, but recurring mental illness made practise impossible. The poetry that he wrote was remarkable. He particularly found solace in the world of nature, and village life. Over the years he attempted suicide many times, but was sustained by his friends through it all. One of his closest friends, John, was a church pastor. John was often called out to help his friend in his distress. John himself wrote hymns that William admired, and the two collaborated on a collection of hymns that were widely used in churches.[236]

William Cowper is now considered one of Britain's greatest poets. John Newton had been a hardened slave trader, before his conversion to Christ. His most famous hymn, still sung around the world, is 'Amazing Grace.' John's persistent care for his friend helped William to come through many periods of depression and several suicide attempts. His poetry is still in print more than two hundred years after it was written.

What can we learn from John Newton's commitment to his friend? Do you tend to avoid 'high maintenance' friendships? If so, do you know why that is? Why is committed friendship a mark of the Christian?

Afterword

Our purpose in this book has been to present Jesus' vision of a radical new community where loyalty to Jesus and love for one another are the hallmarks. We have seen it as the one viable alternative to the loneliness, the isolation and the dysfunction of our modern society. You might well ask where such a community is to be found. Jesus formed his followers into a new society we call the 'church': the Greek word for church is *ecclesia*. It is formed of two words, meaning 'to call' and 'out of'. The church is the society of those 'called out of the world and called together to form the community of the King'.

Some will be quick to point out the failures of the church. After centuries of purity and persecution she succumbed to the legitimacy she was given and became institutionalised. Her leaders formed a hierarchy and became preoccupied with the trappings of power and prestige. At times she has forgotten that she represents 'another country' and has become bogged down in the politics of this 'present evil age'. Instead of representing 'another King, one Jesus' she has sided with the petty rulers of this world. The church's crimes are writ large upon the popular consciousness. And for those of us who

live and work within the orbit of local churches, the petti-
ness and petulance of its people have left their scars on
our memories and families. I cannot but agree with Luther
who said 'the face of the church is the face of a sinner.'

Yet Scripture says that Christ loves the church and I
confess that I love her too. Let me confess unreservedly
her faults and even her cruelties. I grieve over the way in
which she has often surrendered the dynamism of the
biblical vision for religious ideology and institutional-
ism. As Søren Kierkegaard said: 'the most dreadful sort
of blasphemy is that of which Christendom is guilty:
transforming the Spirit of God into ... ludicrous
twaddle'.

But let me also say that there is no other hope for the
world than the church. No other society approximates to
the vision of Jesus we have been exploring in this book
other than the holy, catholic church. In the beginning
Jesus constituted his followers with two decisive words:
'Follow me.' At this point there was no institution, no
hierarchy, no constitution with its rules and regulations,
no code of practice, and no consistory, only his call and
their following.

As Os Guinness puts it in one of his books,[237] the ideas
of calling and following both suggest the idea of a journey. And the very notion of a journey implies something
that is incomplete. The people of God are on their way to
the destination Jesus has mapped out for them. When we
arrive (when he returns) we will be perfect. Becoming
like him in body and soul, we shall be able to love perfectly, relate perfectly and understand each other
perfectly.

The fellowship of the King is his provision to get us to
that ultimate destination. Along the way our relationships
will be tested to the limits. We live out our lives as Jesus-
followers in a war zone of competing ideologies and

corrupting influences from both within and without. If we are to succeed in our mission, we will need each other.

J. R. R. Tolkien did not write allegory but he did write from a Christian world-view. Christian themes pervade the book *Lord of the Rings* and one of the greatest themes is that of 'fellowship'. We see this fellowship at work in the help Frodo receives on his journey; the wisdom of Gandalf (whose sagacity, not his magic, was his greatest power), the aid of a loyal company (the Fellowship of the Ring, the original band of brothers), and the undying love of a slow-witted but great-hearted best friend (Sam Gamgee, the lovable assistant who would have slain a dragon for Frodo, if he didn't trip over his own feet trying).

But there are three other factors in the story that lead to ultimate success: something 'internal' in the character of the main participants; an overarching 'providence' that seems to order events and a regular display of what we might call 'grace': undeserved favour.

The qualities of love and loyalty and justice and mercy enable Frodo Baggins the Hobbit to undertake the most difficult quest in the history of the Third Age of Middle Earth, a task which the most powerful good beings of that era could never have managed – not Aragorn, not Gandalf, not Elrond, nor Galadriel. Because the greatest power of evil was not the external evil of Sauron, but the internal evil that could be unleashed by the use, even for ostensibly good ends, of the one Ring.

We see a pervasive, unnamed divine providence working all things for good; sending Gandalf back from death, putting Gollum at the right place at the right time at Mt. Doom, and leading the ring to be found by Bilbo Baggins in the first place ('the strangest event in the whole history of the ring').

And when in the end, the temptation is too much, even for Frodo, it is only mercy that spares him. Bilbo's original mercy to Gollum, Gandalf's counsel about mercy to Frodo, Frodo's mercy to Gollum, all leave Gollum alive to be the one who, at last, destroys the ring (without intending to!) In the final analysis, Middle Earth is saved from Sauron by grace. None of the characters could have done it. It took divine intervention.

My belief in the church as God's new society is fortified by these three convictions:

I believe in God's Spirit implanted in the believer to fight daily with our old selfish and sinful nature and to arouse within us love for God and love for our neighbour, our enemy and our brother. Such a work is supernatural and is only of God. Any love, loyalty, justice or mercy we are able to show come from this presence deep within the Christ-follower. As with Frodo, such character cannot thrive without the fellowship of the King, the presence of others to cheer us on; to rebuke us and encourage us on our journey.

And I believe in God's grace, the undeserved mercy that seeks us out in the first place and puts us into Christ; the mercy that forgives us when we forget whom we serve and start serving ourselves; the mercy that takes us as we are and begins slowly to address the wrongs in our lives until (sometimes almost imperceptibly) we change into the likeness of Jesus. Whenever I come across a particularly difficult saint, I imagine what they must have been like without Christ! Indeed, when I look into my own heart, I despair of what I would have been without his restraining grace at work in me. God's work in me and in all his people is very much a work in progress.

Finally, I believe in God's providence, that is, his good government of this world. He takes our foolishness and our mistakes and over-rules them to accomplish his purposes. When Jesus said, 'I will build my church', he meant it! He puts the church in the world to be to every age the promise of a new age, a new dawn for humanity when people from every tribe and tongue and culture come to sit down together at a great dinner; where the fruit grows profusely that brings healing to the nations and where all Christ's people join finally together with one heart and one voice to speak the praises of him who called them out of darkness into marvellous light.

Bibliography

Bowlby, J., *Attachment and Loss* (New York, Basic Books, 1969)

Carson, D.A., *For the Love of God*, Vol. I, (Leicester: Inter-Varsity Press, 1998)

Dodd C.H., *The Johannine Epistles* (London: Hodder and Stoughton, 1946)

Doig, Desmond, *Mother Teresa – Her People and Her Work* (London: Collins, 1976)

Kidner, Derek, *Proverbs* (London: Tyndale Press, 1969)

Larson, Bruce, *Dare to Live Now!* (Evesham: Arthur James, 1967)

Law, Robert, *The Tests of Life* (Grand Rapids, Michigan: Baker Book House)

Lee, David, and Schluter, Michael, *The 'R' Factor* (London: Hodder and Stoughton, 1993)

Lloyd-Jones, D.M., *Romans, an exposition of chapter 12: Christian conduct* (Edinburgh: The Banner of Truth, 2000)

Luther, Martin, *Galatians* (London: James Clarke & Co. Ltd, 1953)

Luther, Martin, *Works*, Vol. 53 (Philadelphia: Fortress Press, 1965)

Lynch, J.J., *The broken heart: The medical consequences of loneliness* (New York: Basic Books, 1977)

McCann, Graham, *Woody Allen, New Yorker* (Polity Press, 1990)

Macdonald, M.E., *The Need to Believe*, (London: Fontana, 1959)

Milne, Bruce, *No Longer Alone* (Downers Grove: InterVarsity Press, 1978)

Moustakas, Clark, *Loneliness* (Englewood Cliffs: Prentice-Hall, 1961)

Murray, Andrew, *The Lord's Supper* (Moody Press, 1962)

Naisbitt, John and Aburdene, Patricia, *Megatrends 2000: Ten New Directions for the 1990s* (New York: William Morrow and Co., 1990)

Neighbour, Ralph, *Where Do We Go from Here?* (Touch Publications, 1990)

Neill, Stephen, *Christian Faith Today* (Pelican, 1955)

Ostrov, E. & Offer, D., – Loneliness and the Adolescent. In J. Hartog, J.R. Audy, & Y.A. Cohen (Eds.), *The Anatomy of Loneliness* (New York: International Universities Press, 1980) pp. 170-185

Packer, James I. *Words* (Fearn: Christian Focus, 1998)

Philip, James, *Christian Maturity* (London: Inter-Varsity Press, 1964)

Putnam, Robert D., *Bowling Alone* (New York: Simon & Schuster, 2000)

R.E.M. *Automatic for the People* (album) (R.E.M./Athens Ltd)

Rubinstein, C. & Shaver, P., 'The experience of loneliness', In L.A. Peplau & D. Perlman (Eds.), *Loneliness: a sourcebook of current theory, research and therapy* (New York: John Wiley & Sons, 1982)

Scougal, Henry, *The Life of God in the Soul of Man* (Fearn: Christian Focus, 1996)

Spitz, Rene, *No and Yes: on the Genesis of Human Communication* (New York: International Universities Press, 1957)

Stedman, Ray C., *Body Life* (Regal Books, 1972)

Stott, John. *The Contemporary Christian* (Leicester: Inter-Varsity Press, 1992)

Stott, John. *The Message of Galatians* (London: Inter-Varsity Press, 1968)

Stott, John. *One People* (London: Falcon Books, 1968).

Wesley, John. *Works*, Vol. VIII

'The World's Urban Explosion', in *National Geographic* (August 1984, No. 166, 2)

Endnotes

1. Putnam, Robert D, *Bowling Alone*
2. Putnam, Robert D, *Bowling Alone*
3. Lee, David and Michael Schluter, *The 'R' Factor*
4. 1 John. 1:3
5. See 'Lost in the Crowd', *The Big Issue*, July 1-7, 2002, No. 495
6. Although the saying was attributed to Garbo, she always insisted that she had only said, 'I want to be left alone.' The same line was later said by her in the film, *Grand Hotel*
7. Bowlby, J., *Attachment and Loss*
8. Spitz, Rene, *No and Yes: on the Genesis of Human Communication*
9. Lynch, J. J., *The Broken Heart: The Medical Consequences of Loneliness*
10. Ostrov, E. & Offer, D. (1980) – *Loneliness and the Adolescent*. In J. Hartog, J.R. Audy, & Y.A. Cohen (Eds.), *The Anatomy of Loneliness*, pp. 170-185
11. Sue Sainsbury, in *Evangelicals Now*
12. As the world population continues to explode, life on earth is becoming increasingly metropolitan: the number of cities with a population exceeding five million people mushroomed from seven in 1950 to thirty-four in 1984, and is forecast to reach ninety-three by the year 2025. 'The World's Urban Explosion,' *National Geographic*

[13] August 28th, 1995

[14] The proportion of single people buying their own home rose from 25 per cent in 1983 to 41 per cent in 2001, according to the Halifax Group, August 2002

[15] Lee, David and Michael Schluter, *The R Factor*

[16] For example, C. Rubinstein and P. Shaver, The experience of loneliness' in *Loneliness: a sourcebook of current theory, research and therapy*, pp206-223

[17] This is especially the case in our Western culture, which encourages the belief that romantic love will solve every problem. Often, having married our dream person, we destroy our love by expecting too much of it. In the end, our spouse cannot meet all our needs, we have left our family and old friends behind, we have lost our dream and, now, we feel very much alone

[18] M.E. Macdonald, *The need to believe*, p82

[19] Clark Moustakas, *Loneliness*

[20] C.H. Dodd, Moffatt, *Commentary on the Johannine Epistles*

[21] 2 Timothy 4:2

[22] John 1:1-2

[23] John 14:6. See also John1:4

[24] John 5:25-26

[25] John 11:25

[26] John 11:44

[27] I John 1:3

[28] Deuteronomy 6:4. Known as the *Shema*, Hebrew for 'Hear', it has become the Jewish confession of faith, recited daily by the pious.

[29] John 1:1-3

[30] Genesis 1:2

[31] Genesis 1:3

[32] Genesis 1:26, emphasis mine. Some have argued that the 'us' is a plural of majesty, like Queen Victoria saying, 'We are not amused.' However, the Hebrew form does not allow this interpretation.

33 John 17:1

34 John 17:24-26

35 Genesis 2:18

36 D.A. Carson, *For the Love of God*, *Vol. I*, commentary on January 2

37 See John 15:1-8

38 2 Peter 1:4 (emphasis mine)

39 Galatians 2:20

40 Henry Scougal, *The life of God in the soul of man*. Scougal lived 1650-1678.

41 John 17:5, 21

42 1 John 1:3

43 John 1:12,13

44 Romans 8:15

45 I John 4:13

46 Galatians 4:8-9

47 Romans 11:33-36

48 I John 1:7

49 John 17:3

50 1 John 2:23

51 John 1:12

52 2 John 9

53 John 14:23

54 I John 4:10

55 Leviticus 16:21

56 Hebrews 10:4

57 Hebrews 10:1

58 John 1:29

59 1 John 4:9

60 1 John 4:13

61 Acts 2: 38

62 Acts 2:36

63 Acts 2:38

64 Romans 8:9

65 I John 3:24

66 I John 2:20

67 For example, see Galatians 2:20, Romans 6:1, Ephesians 1:3 and 2 Timothy 2:12.

68 The 'earnest' refers to the help of the Holy Spirit

69 Romans 8:35-37

70 1 John 2:15-17

71 1 John 3:10

72 1 John 1:9

73 Graham McCann, *Woody Allen, New Yorker*, p222

74 Desmond Doig, *Mother Teresa – Her People and Her Work*, p159

75 John 13:34-35

76 Romans 12:10

77 I John 1:4

78 I John 4:7

79 I John 4: 8,16.

80 For example by Robert Law, in *The Tests of Life*

81 John 4:24

82 I John 1:5

83 1 John 4:7

84 I John 4:9-12

85 Ephesians 2:1,4-5

86 John 5:25

87 I John 4:9

88 2 Corinthians 9:15

89 1 John 4:10

90 Galatians 2:20

91 Genesis 22:1-19

92 Romans 8:32

93 1 John 4:12

94 Isaiah 6:1

95 See especially Ezekiel 1

96 Exodus 33:20

97 1 John 4:11

98 1 John 3:18

99 John 13:35

[100] John 15:12
[101] Matthew 5:46-47
[102] 1 John 4:19
[103] 1 John 4:21
[104] 1 Corinthians 13:13
[105] 1 Corinthians 13:4-8.
[106] James I. Packer, *Words*, p193.
[107] Romans 12:5.
[108] Romans 12:10.
[109] Ephesians 1:7
[110] Ephesians2:19.
[111] Romans 8:15.
[112] D.M. Lloyd-Jones, *Romans*, p351.
[113] Romans 15:7.
[114] Romans 14:13.
[115] Romans 14:5.
[116] Galatians 5:15, 26.
[117] Colossians 3:9.
[118] James 4:11; 5:9.
[119] Ephesians 4:2,32]
[120] Ephesians 4: 32.
[121] Romans 14: 15.
[122] Romans 15:1.
[123] Ephesians 4:32.
[124] Ephesians 4:2.
[125] 1 Peter 4:9.
[126] Galatians 5:13.
[127] John 13:1-3.
[128] 1 Peter 4:10
[129] Romans 15:14.
[130] Galatians 6:2.
[131] 1 Thessalonians 4:18.
[132] 1 John 3:18.
[133] Galatians 6:2.
[134] Ephesians 4:12

135 1 Corinthians 12:25
136 Galatians 6:2; 1 Thessalonians 5:14; Romans 15:1
137 1 Corinthians 2:3.
138 2 Corinthians 1:8.
139 2 Corinthians 4:8-9
140 2 Corinthians 12:5-9
141 Romans1: 12; 2 Corinthians 7:6
142 Bruce Milne, *No Longer Alone*, pp75, 76
143 Hebrews 2:17
144 Hebrews. 4:15
145 James 5:16
146 Bruce Milne, *No Longer Alone*, p81
147 James 5:16
148 Psalms 139:1-4
149 John Naisbitt and Patricia Aburdene, *Megatrends 2000: Ten New Directions for the 1990s*
150 Lee, David, and Schluter Michael, *The R Factor*
151 Hebrews 10:25
152 Hebrews 3:13
153 1 Samuel 23:16
154 See Acts 11
155 Acts 4:36
156 1Thessalonians 2:11-12; 5:11
157 Hebrews10:25
158 Acts 2:42
159 John Stott, *The Contemporary Christian*, p235
160 Stephen C. Neill, *Christian Faith Today*, p174.
161 Acts 2:46-47
162 Matthew10:9-11; Luke 10:8-11
163 Romans12:13
164 1 Peter 4:9
165 Bruce Larson, *Dare to Live Now!* p110
166 2 Corinthians1:3,4
167 1 John 4:16-18
168 Matthew 18:20

169 Proverbs 27:17
170 Ecclesiastes 4:9-10
171 John 15:14
172 Proverbs 18 :24
173 Genesis 2:24
174 Ruth 1:14
175 Deuteronomy 10:20; 11:22
176 Derek Kidner, *Proverbs*, p44
177 John 15:15
178 Proverbs 15:31
179 Acts 2:46
180 J. R. W. Stott, *One People*, p70
181 Joel 2:25, RSV
182 Matthew 9:12,13
183 Titus 3:5
184 Galatians 5:26-6:2
185 2 Corinthians 7:5-6
186 Galatians 6:1
187 John 8:4
188 Mark 1:19
189 John Stott, *The Message of Galatians*, p160
190 Martin Luther, *Galatians*, p538
191 Galatians 6:1
192 Galatians 5:18,22,25
193 James Philip, *Christian Maturity*, p66
194 Galatians 6:1
195 Matthew 26:70,72
196 John 21
197 James 5:19-20
198 Luke 22:17,18
199 Corinthians 11:26
200 Romans 3:10-12
201 Ezekiel 18:4
202 Romans 6:23
203 Genesis 2:16-17

204 Genesis 3:21

205 1 Corinthians 10:16-17

206 1 Corinthians 11:24

207 Andrew Murray, *The Lord's Supper*, p84

208 1 Corinthians 5:7

209 Matthew 5:23-24

210 Colossians 3:13

211 1 Peter 3:11

212 Darija Stojnic, 'Guess who's coming to dinner?' in *The Big Issue* (August 5-11, 2002), p20

213 Ray C. Stedman, *Body Life*, p108

214 Colossians 1:18

215 Martin Luther, *Works*, Vol. 53, 63

216 John Wesley, *Works*, Vol. VIII, p299

217 John Wesley, *Works*, Vol. VIII, p251-252

218 John Wesley, *Works*, Vol. VIII, p272.

219 See Ralph Neighbour, *Where do we go from here?*

220 Hebrews 12:15

221 Proverbs 25:19

222 2 Timothy 4:16

223 Proverbs 27:10

224 Proverbs 15:22; 20:18

225 Proverbs 12:15;19:20

226 Proverbs 27:5-6

227 Proverbs 15:31-32

228 Proverbs 17:9

229 Jeremiah 31:34

230 1 John 1:7

231 Ecclesiastes 4:9-10

232 Ecclesiastes 4:11

233 Ecclesiastes 4:12

234 Proverbs 17:17

235 John 15:12-13,15

236 For more information see: www.mkheritage.co.uk/cnm/index.html

[237] Os Guinness, *The Call* (Carlisle, Spring Harvest publishing, 2002)